Hope f

[handwritten inscription:]

Luke!

God Bless You!

Hope Filled Reading!

Pastor Hubert

By
Hubert Nolen

Table of Contents

Dedication

To my wife, Tonia, who supported me through the writing process of this book and patiently typed the first manuscript. We have shared every hope moment in this book, and in our most hopeless moments, together we turned our eyes to Christ, Who gave us hope to face another day. I look forward to the rest of our lives serving Christ together and experiencing His hope for a lifetime.

Timeline

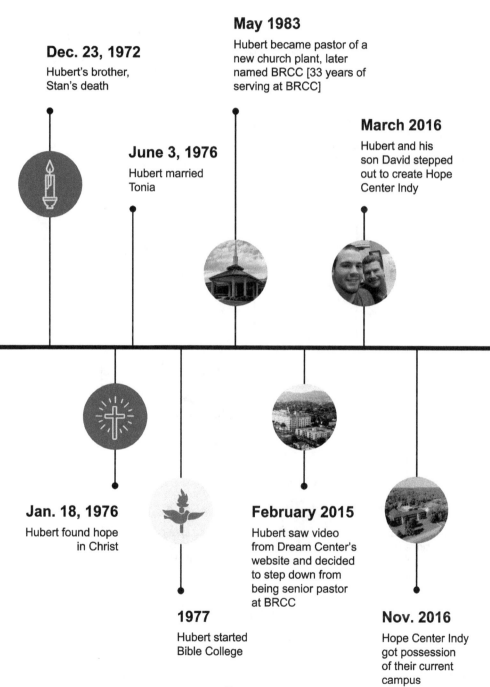

Dec. 23, 1972
Hubert's brother,
Stan's death

May 1983
Hubert became pastor of a
new church plant, later
named BRCC [33 years of
serving at BRCC]

June 3, 1976
Hubert married
Tonia

March 2016
Hubert and his
son David stepped
out to create Hope
Center Indy

Jan. 18, 1976
Hubert found hope
in Christ

February 2015
Hubert saw video
from Dream Center's
website and decided
to step down from
being senior pastor
at BRCC

1977
Hubert started
Bible College

Nov. 2016
Hope Center Indy
got possession
of their current
campus

2017

Hope Center Indy began hiring their first program staff

August 2017

HCI opened residential program for survivors of sex trafficking

May 2019

Hubert's son David's Death

February 2022

Completed K9 Barn on campus for Jordan K9 Detection

May 2020

IMPD search warrant

May 2017

HCI started boutique as an ongoing fundraiser

October 2019

Hubert's daughter Mary hired as new HCI Associate Director

March 2018

HCI opened wedding venue as an ongoing wedding venue

January 2021

Case against HCI was closed and no charges filed

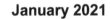

1

Needing Hope

Maybe you picked up this book because you have heard about Hope Center Indy. Today Hope Center Indy sits on a 25-acre campus in Indianapolis and provides residential care for women overcoming sex trafficking, sexual exploitation, and addictions. Hope Center Indy's mission statement is to "impart hope and healing to every heart." Alongside our thirty local and national partners, our staff's goal is to impart hope to our residents and the people we serve in our community every day through our compassion ministries. But I want to rewind the story to share with you how the Lord prepared me to start this wonderful organization. My story starts at the age of seventeen when tragedy struck my family, and as a young man, I went searching for the hope I so desperately needed. Hope often shows up as a small flicker of light in our darkest moments.

Hope for a Lifetime is my story of seeking God's hope in every challenge. I want you to know my family and I have lived every part of this book. Every chapter of my life has been saturated with prayer as I have asked for my heavenly Father to guide my steps through a wonderful life journey with Him. We all have suffered losses and heart-wrenching moments. While writing this paragraph, I received a phone call from a dear friend. He was crying. He had just received the tragic news that his friend had just died, and he was driving to his friend's house to be with his widow and children. Through his brokenness and tears, he asked for prayer for himself and this dear family. He was praying not only for comfort, but also for hope to rise above their loss.

All of us have received a phone call like this before—bad news about an accident, cancer, divorce, relapse, the company downsizing that means you will lose your job, etc. It is in these moments we want to quit on life. But I want to encourage you—don't quit. Never give up. The hope you so desperately need and are searching for is freely available. I will share in this book about my wife and I going through our biggest heartache of losing our son David when he was twenty-eight. It is in the darkness of tragedy that the God of all comfort and hope comes to meet us and remove the feelings of despair and overwhelming hopelessness. As we turn our eyes away from our problems and look up, we can experience the power of hope.

It is our prayer that you might experience the same life-changing hope we have received as a family. We pray that you will not only find hope to survive another day, but that you will desire to dream big. Hope is the foundation for you—a springboard for you to live your life in abundance and joyful purpose with your heavenly Father.

I have tried to put the chapters in chronological order, but this was difficult because life unfolds daily with multiple things happening at the same time. I'm providing a timeline of my life and Hope Center Indy's beginnings at the front of this book for you to refer to as you read the stories. I pray that this helps you realize how our lives are made up of small steps of obedience which lead to greater steps that lead us down the pathway of hope.

The Phone Call

On December 23, 1972, I was seventeen and had arrived home late from a date. I had just gone to sleep when I could lightly hear the phone ringing in the other room. Little did I know that from that moment forward, my life would never be the same. The next thing I knew my mom was screaming, "Stan's had a wreck. Stan's had a wreck." Stan was my older brother, four years older, just twenty-one. I had shared a bedroom with Stan for most of my life. He was the one I would play basketball with. I loved to laugh at his jokes; he was the funny one in our family.

I don't know if you have ever been awakened by someone screaming, but when I heard my mom's screams, I had to sit up in bed and think, *Where am I? What's going on?*

I got out of bed and started toward my mom. In 1972 we had a rotary dial phone. I saw the receiver was dangling by the stand.

When I reached my mom, I tried to calm her, but nothing I said was helping. She was crying and screaming, "Stan's been in a wreck!" My dad had gotten out of bed and went straight to the phone.

I was now standing by my dad, listening. I thought, "Okay, Stan's been in a wreck. We will go to the hospital. Maybe he will be there for a few days. The doctors will start him on the pathway to healing, and we will bring him home. He will get well."

But the next words I heard my dad say were, "I guess we will have his body taken to Hampton's Mortuary." Those words turned my world inside out and upside down. I now knew what my mom had already known. All I could do was go to my bedroom, fall on my bed, and cry—cry out to God if He was there. For the first time in my life, I felt hopelessness and despair.

As a child, I went to church a few times. My family believed that God was there, that there was a place called "heaven," and we were taught right from wrong. But I didn't know answers to important faith questions: What does it mean to accept Jesus as my Savior? What does it mean to be born again? What does the Bible say about how I become a Christian? And when I die, is eternal life awaiting all who believe?

For the first time in my life, I was directly confronted with death. My oldest brother Allen's wife and unborn child had tragically died a few years before this, but I had been able to block out the heartache because she had been part of our family for only a few years. Because of my young age, I never fully comprehended the loss he experienced. This time I could not block out the pain because Stan had been so close to me—a constant part of my childhood, a role model I admired and loved. As a family, we didn't have a small group, a church family, or a class like Grief Share to help us work through our loss. My mom would cry at the supper table. Dad would mostly be silent because he didn't know how to comfort her. He was carrying his own heartache and was trying to be strong for Mom. My parents, my brothers and sisters, and I each dealt with our grief over losing Stan in our own way. My way was to try not to think about it because the sorrow and pain I felt were too intense when I did. At age seventeen, I couldn't identify my own feelings of grief, and I hurt for the pain I saw in my parents.

As a young teenager living in rural Indiana, I had worked every summer baling hay and mowing lawns. I then worked at a local restaurant as a bus boy, washing dishes to save money to buy my first car. I had bought Stan's 1968 Dodge Charger for $1,000. Stan had wanted to sell me the car because he had just returned from the service and gotten married. He used the money to purchase a home for his new bride. I was excited to have my own car and proud of my purchase. I drove to school every day because I participated in sports. I played football, basketball, and track. I had always been eager to work hard, improve, and learn from successful people. But now it was like a dark cloud hovered over my life. Inside I felt empty, and I had lost my desire to achieve. I realized that I needed something more than having a cool car or playing sports to make me happy, but I didn't know what could bring me healing and purpose. I now realize I was fighting depression, but as a teenager, I was overwhelmed with grief and didn't know where to look for help. So I did what many people do: I looked for comfort in alcohol, drugs, and anything that would take away my dead feeling inside.

Indiana State University

After my brother's death, I remembered a conversation I had had with him only a few months before he passed. My brother had gotten a job straight out of high school. It was good money, but he didn't like it. He said to me, "Don't do what I've done. Go to college and get your degree and do what you want to do!" So, as I was making plans for what I would do after high school, I could remember Stan saying, "Go to college and get your degree. Do what you want to do." So I enrolled at Indiana State University (made famous by one of my favorite basketball players Larry Bird in 1979). We called Indiana State at Terre Haute "Sin City" because it had a party atmosphere that rivaled any other college campus across America. Even though I went to college hoping to find purpose and better myself, I was faced with a lot of temptation. I tried to do what Stan wanted me to do, but I soon found that I didn't have the willpower.

When I arrived at college, my brother's death was only nine months in the rearview mirror. By the time I made it halfway through the first semester of my sophomore year, I had totally given up on getting a college degree. I was studying finance, but somehow I knew this was not my lot in life. So I stopped going to class and limped toward the finish line of that semester. I knew I was going to flunk almost all of my classes. I remember thinking, "My mom and dad work too hard for me to party away my education

7

and waste their money." My dad worked at a factory, and my mom worked at the local hospital cafeteria. They were still raising my younger brother at home and did not have money for me to waste. So, I decided to wait on continuing college. I thought, "If I can ever figure out what I want to do with my life, I will go back to college and get my degree. But what I am doing right now is a waste of time and money."

I got a job driving an oil truck, delivering fuel for J.R. Wortman Company to farmers and home heating oil to other customers. One day, on a delivery at a local farm, I was impressed with the farmer's setup. He had a farrow to finish hog operation, some acreage to grow corn, and a nice farmhouse. Each day to go to work, he just walked out his door and down to the barn to do his chores. I thought, I would love to work for myself like that someday.

When I gave the farmer his ticket for fuel, I told him I would be interested in buying his farm if he ever wanted to sell it. To my surprise, he said, "What would you give me?"

Without thinking, I said a number off the top of my head.

He smiled and said, "If I ever want to sell, I'll keep you in mind."

Several months later, he called and wanted me to come over because he had something to discuss. I had not given our previous conversation any thought over the past several months, but as I drove to his house, I thought, Surely he's not interested in selling his farm. When I arrived, we sat down at their kitchen table.

After greeting each other, he said, "I've found a farm I want to buy, so I am going to call your bluff. I want you to buy mine." I must have looked a little overwhelmed, so he asked, "What do you need to do?"

I said, "I guess I need to see if I can borrow enough money to buy the farm."

He said, "Okay. Take your time and see what you can do."

After I left their home, I thought, How crazy is this? A nineteen-year-old trying to buy a farm!

I sat down and put together a cash flow chart on how I was going to pay for the hog farm. I had learned this in my college finance classes. (So at least those classes were good for something!) I showed how many hogs I could raise with the projected profit, the corn crop I could raise with its projected profit, and my income from my job driving an oil delivery truck. I put all this on a spreadsheet, and I made an appointment with the banker. As I was walking up the sidewalk to the bank, I prayed. I am not sure why because I hadn't been praying much, but in that moment, I prayed, God, if you want me to get this farm, let this happen. If not, I don't want it to go through.

As I entered his office, I sat down, took out my spreadsheets, and placed them on his desk. He began to look at my plan, and he didn't even ask me any questions. He studied them for what seemed like an eternity, but it was probably only about five to ten minutes. He finally looked up at me and said, "You think you can do this, don't you?"

"I do."

"So do I. I will go to bat for you and see if we can get this done."

He did get it done. Even though I was only nineteen years old, the bank loaned me the money, and I moved into the farmhouse in September of 1975.

Good News from Morris

I had a friend at work, Morris, who was going through some financial problems—or maybe I should say he was going through some life problems. He was partying away his paycheck every week and not paying his bills. He got an eviction notice, and his truck was being repossessed. He said to me one day, "Hey, could I move in with you?"

I said, "You and me together, that's bad news. I don't think that would be a good idea."

But several days later, as I was thinking about his plight, I felt prompted to tell him he could move in. Little did I know this would be a life-changing decision! My fears became a reality. All we did was party. I started missing work because I was hungover. I began to feel that my life and the

10

opportunity I had been given with the farm were starting to slip away.

On December 28, 1975, Morris invited some friends to the farm for a party. We had a lot of snow that winter, so Morris left early to take his date home. A little later, as I was taking my date home, I came upon a police car with its lights flashing. As we got closer, I could tell it was Morris' truck the police had stopped. I wasn't concerned because back then the local police who knew you would make sure you could drive safely and follow you home. They would simply say, "Don't let me catch you drinking and driving again." (Times have changed, haven't they?)

When I got home later from taking my date home, the party was still going on. The friends had stayed. I walked in and said, "Hey, where is Morris? I didn't see his truck."

They said, "He is in the Shelby County Jail." I can't remember how his bail was posted, but the next day he came home. When he walked into the house, I noticed he looked different. His countenance had changed.

His cousin said, "Morris, can I fix you a drink?"

"No, man. I don't want a drink."

"What jail cell were you in?"

"The second one on the left."

His cousin joked, "That's the one I was in!"

Again, I noticed that something was different about Morris. He didn't laugh at his cousin's remark or make light

11

of the situation. He walked through the kitchen and went upstairs to get his stuff and left for the rest of the weekend. I didn't see him again until Monday after work.

When I got home from work, Morris said, "Let's run to town and get something to eat."

As we jumped in my truck and backed out of the driveway to head out, Morris struck up a conversation about his weekend. "I was at this family's home over the weekend, and they started telling me everything God was doing in the lives of people!"

At first I did a double take. He had been in jail on Saturday and was talking to me about God on Monday. For some strange reason, those things did not add up to me. But the more he talked, the more I felt a welling up of joy inside. I was so excited to hear that God was alive and that He cared about us. All the way to the restaurant and back home, we talked about God, mostly in our ignorance, because neither of us knew much about Him.

About a mile from home, Morris said, "So what are you going to do about it?"

I said, "Do about what?"

"What we have been discussing."

"I want to change. I want to stop all this party life," I said.

Morris asked, "Would you go to church with me Sunday?"

"Sure, no big deal." I thought, I can sit in the back and clean out my billfold or something.

My first morning at church for years was not at all what I had expected. A young couple sang a song. I don't remember anything from the song, except the phrase "open your spiritual eyes and see." There I was, twenty years old, sitting in Little Blue River Friends Church, and as they sang, I got a big lump in my throat. My eyes filled with tears. I thought, *I can't cry in a church.*

The pastor gave a good message, and at the end, he said, "If you are here today and want to receive Christ, come to an altar of prayer, and I will pray with you."

I thought, *Receive Christ? What does that mean?*

The next Sunday, Morris and I went to church again. Again after the sermon, the pastor said, "If you would like to receive Christ, I will pray with you." I still could not understand how anyone could receive Christ. It sounded strange and confusing to someone who had not read the Bible.

On Wednesday night, January 18, 1976, I went to bed. As I lay down, I thought about praying. I wanted to pray to God, but the only problem was I didn't know how. I didn't know what to pray to receive Jesus or what to ask of God to receive salvation. I didn't know how to pray a sinner's prayer. That night I said a very simple but earnest prayer. I said, "God, will you take my life?"

Wow! When I prayed that, I felt this amazing cleansing feeling, a warmth in my heart and life. It only lasted thirty seconds or so, but I remember thinking how wonderful it felt. Isn't it wonderful that God hears the cry of our hearts? It wasn't the eloquence of the words of my prayer; it was the sincerity of my faith that pleased God and brought forth salvation.

The next day as I headed to work, something was different. The world looked clean, like I was seeing it with opened spiritual eyes. Over the next week or so, my desires changed. I wanted to read the Bible, go to church, and learn as much as I could. The old me with my old habits was passing away, and a brand-new me had come to life. I had been given a new birth (John 3:3), a new heart, and a new spirit (Ezekiel 36:26).

I had become a new creation, as Paul says in 2 Corinthians 5:17. Being this new person in Christ didn't mean I wouldn't ever sin again—just that this new me had other desires. I wanted to live for God and not for myself. Instantly, swear words stopped coming out of my mouth. I lost most of my vocabulary that day. I found my pocket-sized Gideon Bible, which had been given to me in grade school. It replaced the cigarettes I had carried in my shirt pocket. Before, I had never praised Jesus. I had only used His name in vain. Now He was all I wanted to talk about. I had a new zeal, a fire on the inside. I wanted everyone to know the joy, the peace, and the love of God flowing from my new heart.

After seeing the change in me, another friend and coworker said I was a "unicorn." He meant that I was something you never see! One day I was this old me, and the next day I was a brand-new me. He couldn't grasp such a life change, even though I shared my wonderful life-changing moment with him. There was a new Hubert Nolen, and God had begun a good work in him (Philippians 2:13). I was excited to see all God had in store.

Just Ask

I don't even know how many times I have shared my story with others. After I am finished, people often ask me about Morris. The night Morris was put in jail, he said he was thinking about how he had let his mom and dad down. He had let everyone who had ever believed in him down. As he was having this heart-searching moment, it was like Jesus said, "Morris, look around this cell. I have something better for you to do."

At that moment, a peace fell over him, and he fell asleep. The next day when he came home, he looked different because he was different. Christ had changed him in jail. The guy who was bad news brought me the good news of the gospel!

When I share my story, I often ask, "Do you want to know where Morris is today?"

When they nod, I tell them he is back in jail. Their smiles drop. You can almost hear a groan or two. Then I say, "No, he is not! He went on to get his doctorate and has been pastoring for over forty years. The Lord did a good work when He created a new Morris."

I am reminded that my journey to find hope started with the tragic death of my brother Stan. Even though at times, I searched in all the wrong places, I finally found the hope I was looking for in the person of Jesus. I am no special person. What God did for me on that night in 1976, He will do for all who desire to know Him and give their lives to Him. You too can become a new creation in Christ. You too can receive a new heart and a new spirit. All you have to do is ask! You can find in Him the hope that you have been needing.

Promises to Read:

Ezekiel 36:26: "I will give you a new heart and put a new spirit in you; I will remove from you your heart of stone and give you a heart of flesh."

John 3:3: "Jesus replied, 'Very truly I tell you, no one can enter the kingdom of God unless they are born of water and the Spirit.'"

2 Corinthians 5:17: "Therefore, if anyone is in Christ, the new creation has come. The old has gone, the new is here!"

Prayer to Pray:

Lord Jesus, I believe You are the Christ, the Son of our loving, heavenly Father. I ask You to forgive me of my sins, take my life, and be my Savior and Lord. I want to be born again and receive a new heart and a new spirit! I want to be a new creation in You! Give me the gift of your salvation and the hope of everlasting life.

In Jesus' name, I ask for all these things, Amen.

2

From the Pig Pen to the Pulpit

As a new Christian at the age of twenty, I knew little about the Bible, church, or God's work. I was an unlikely candidate to be called by God, but I remember almost begging God if I could serve Him in some way. I was willing to serve in any way He could use me. I hadn't yet learned Jesus' words that the harvest was plentiful and the workers were few, and we were to pray to the Lord of the harvest to send workers into the harvest field (Luke 10:2).

After becoming this new creation, my desires quickly started changing. One day I was standing and looking at this pen of hogs. All of a sudden, it was like I was having a running conversation with Jesus.

Hubert, what do you want to do with your life?

I want to invest in what is eternal.

What is eternal?

Your word and the souls of people.

What about these hogs?

No, they are here six months and then off to the market.

So, what do you want to do with your life?

I want to learn Your word and invest in people.

(Have you ever had a conversation about eternal things like this with the Lord? If not, this kind of prayer dialogue could be life-changing.)

At work, before I set out for deliveries, I would need to fill my delivery truck, which held around 1,500 gallons of fuel, so it took about twenty minutes for the four tanks to fill up. I would read my Gideon Bible while I waited. One day I was praying and asking the Lord, "What do you want me to do for You?"

I was reading in Luke's Gospel chapter 4. As I was reading along, I came to verse 18: "The Spirit of the Lord is on me because He has anointed me to proclaim good news to the poor. He has sent me to proclaim freedom for the prisoners and recovery of sight for the blind, to set the oppressed free." As I read this verse, my eyes filled with tears, the Holy Spirit washed over me, and I knew the Holy Spirit was speaking to me. It was the Holy Spirit bearing witness with my spirit. This verse was for me.

I knew at that moment I was being called to preach the good news of the gospel. This was my invitation to be a worker in the harvest field. Was I willing to say yes? I had the chance to go from raising hogs and growing corn to being a worker in the Lord's harvest field! It was like I had been eagerly expecting this moment, and now I was filled with joy. Little did I realize at that time what my future would bring.

Bible College

I married my high school sweetheart, Tonia Wright, on June 3, 1976. Our first step of faith would be to leave the farm. But hadn't I committed myself to a twenty-year mortgage that would need to be paid off? One Sunday night I was sitting in church, telling the Lord why I couldn't serve Him because of my financial commitment. The Lord gave me a mental picture of my dad sitting in front of the fireplace in my farmhouse. It was like the Lord saying, "This is your answer. Ask your parents to take over the farm. No more excuses."

I was convinced that my parents would never leave their home. But I prayed, "God, if you prepare their hearts, I will ask them."

A few months later, I stopped by my parents' home to visit with them. We were enjoying a cup of coffee when my mom said, "I said to your dad the other day, what are we doing here? Why don't we move or go somewhere else?"

My mouth must have fallen open. I said, "Why don't you wait until this fall, and then you can take over my farm?"

Mom said, "Son, what would you do?"

I said, "I guess I am going into the ministry, and this fall I am heading to Bible college."

That fall Mom and Dad moved to my farm, and Tonia and I headed off to Barclay College, 830 miles away, to a tiny place called Haviland, Kansas. It was said of Haviland that "It wasn't the end of the world, but you could see the end from there." Or maybe just the college kids said that because there was nothing to do except go to school. Thankfully, my friend Morris and his brother Marvin also started at Barclay College the same semester, so we had a sense of family and fellowship there.

My first semester in Bible college was a real eye-opener for me. I hadn't applied myself academically in high school. I'm not proud of it and am almost ashamed to admit it, but if I couldn't bounce it, shoot it, or catch it, I wasn't interested in it. This was something I never wanted my son David to know about me when he was in school. I went to school to play sports, not to learn. One day, when I was late for school, the vice principal stopped me in the hallway. He tried to encourage me to be a leader, to be an example, and to apply myself. After his pep talk, he walked me down to my first period class, which was a study hall. He opened the door and spoke to the study hall teacher, saying I had been with him and didn't need a pass from the office. I entered the classroom and was about halfway to my seat when the vice principal yelled at the top of his voice, "Nolen, get out here!" I'm pretty sure he woke everyone up in study hall that morning. As I walked slowly back to the hallway, I had no idea why he was so angry. (Houston, I didn't know we had a problem.) His face was red, and he was visibly upset. He looked me in the face and said, "Get a book."

I said, "I don't have any books."

He didn't believe me, so he said, "Open your locker."

So we went to my locker. I opened the door as wide as I could, so he could see in. The locker was empty of books; there was just some paper trash at the bottom of my locker. He stood there and stared at my empty locker while his educational life must have passed before him. How could it be that a senior student in his school didn't even own a single book? The truth of the matter is that I did start the year with one book—my government book. But a friend had borrowed it, and I never went looking for it. (Hey, Joe! Give me back my book!) Finally, the vice principal said to me, "Just get in there and sit down." So I did.

As you can tell, my study habits really put me behind when it came to college-level work. In my Old Testament Survey class, one day I was taking a test and had to answer a test question with a short essay that was only one paragraph long. I turned my test in. During the next class, when we got our graded tests back, the professor, Mrs. Mauck, asked if she could speak to me after class. I hung around, and after everyone was gone, she said, "I have been impressed with your spiritual passion and your desire to work to serve Jesus. But your writing skills and your grammar are so bad that you will never make it in ministry." My face must have shown my shock and disappointment. She continued, "But, I tell you what I will do. I will help you. I will meet with you and help you learn."

I began meeting with Mrs. Mauck once a week, and she helped me learn the basic rules of grammar and sentence structure. I remember those sessions on verb tenses and irregular verbs. If Mrs. Mauck hadn't taken the time to help me learn basic writing skills, I doubt I would have been able to finish college or even write sermons (or write a book!). Yet she was obedient to God and used her skills to help build up the body of Christ. Without her, I would have never learned how to communicate effectively. (If you are a teacher, I hope this part of my story reminds you of the impact teachers can have for the kingdom of God! I am so proud of my daughter Shari, who is a middle school teacher and my son-in-law Royce, who is a high school teacher. They view their jobs as teachers as a ministry to invest in young people's lives and influence them for Christ, just like Mrs. Mauck did for me.)

Soon I was shocked to receive a ministry opportunity for which I was the most unlikely candidate. The host church of the Bible college had in its congregation around 25–30 retired pastors, the college president, professors from the college, and a lot of college graduates. Any of them would have been qualified employees for the church and probably would have been excited to serve on the church staff. So you can imagine my surprise, and Mrs. Mauck's, when the senior pastor of the church asked *me*—of all people!—to join the church staff after I had completed only one year of Bible college. I was excited to accept the invitation, and I began working by leading the youth group and preaching sometimes on Sunday mornings. The college president said my first sermon was a grammatical disaster, but I showed great promise.

The church filled with all the pastors and professors loved a young hog farmer. Their words of encouragement, prayers, and willingness to let me learn and fail spurred me on. I realized that the Holy Spirit could use even me to share something from God's word that would minister to their hearts.

One of my last classes in college was a Christian education class. For our final exam, the professor wanted us students to take the principles we had learned in the class and tell him how we would use them to serve the local church. I am not sure why, but I took those principles and wrote a paper on how I would use them to plant a new church. I had never thought about being a church planter, but the paper sure did come together.

The professor never told me, but he told the senior pastor of the church that when he read my paper about planting a church, the Holy Spirit bore witness with him that I was going to do this. As he was reading and sensing the Holy Spirit, he wept over my paper. (My friend Morris said he didn't weep over God's anointing on the vision of a church plant; he wept over my grammar! There may have been some truth in both!) It was like God had put the desire to plant a church in my heart, and He brought it to the surface through this paper.

New Church Plant

I graduated from Barclay College in 1981 and was on staff at the church for another year. During my fifth year on the church staff, I felt I was at a crossroads. Either I was going to stay at the church for a long time, or I needed to head to seminary for more training.

In the fall of 1982, we set out for seminary as a family. Tonia and I already had two daughters, Sara and Rachel who were born while we were at Bible college in Kansas. We ended up at Asbury Seminary in Wilmore, Kentucky. My first year there was wonderful. I learned so much. The professors were an all-star lineup of great men of God: Dr. Robert Coleman, Dr. David Thompson, Dr. Dennis Kinshaw, Dr. David Seamen, and many others. In April of 1983, I started feeling an expectancy in my spirit like something was about to happen. Tonia and I were expecting our third precious daughter, Shari, who would be born in May of 1983. But there also was another expectancy in my spirit.

One day the phone rang, and it was my good friend Dr. Michael Henderson. He asked if I could hold a second, and he put me on hold. At the beginning of my Christian life, Dr. Henderson discipled me for a couple years. He challenged me to memorize Scripture, share my testimony, and begin to invest in others through leading a small group. Now Dr. Henderson was serving at Community Church of Greenwood with Dr. Charles Lake.

While I was on hold, I turned to Tonia and said, "He is going to offer us a ministry opportunity."

I knew that this thought was from God. I had not been expecting his phone call, nor did I have any reason to assume they would want me to go into ministry with them.

When Dr. Henderson came back on the phone, he said, "We have a group of believers on the Eastside of Indianapolis that is trying to plant a church. I wanted to see if you would be interested in leading this church plant."

My first response was, "No, but I'll pray about it." I wanted to finish my Master of Divinity degree. Tonia and I did pray and meet with Dr. Lake, Dr. Henderson, and the leaders of the new church plant. After praying and discussing it, we felt compelled to say yes. At the end of the semester, we loaded up our three daughters and moved back to Indiana to be part of this new church plant.

My first Sunday at Community Christian Fellowship was the first Sunday of August 1983. On our first Sunday, we met in a Seventh-day Adventist building, and we had 50 people. Over the next several months, we quickly grew from 50 to 120 in attendance. I thought, This is fun. This church planting is a piece of cake. But the honeymoon period came to an end, and real life and real ministry started. I struggled to lead, being only twenty-eight years old. Because I lacked experience and the wisdom that comes with age, I found it difficult to gain people's respect and to be confident. Criticism started coming my way. People didn't like my preaching, my theology, my vision, or where I was taking the church. Disunity became the norm. Over the next three years (with my great preaching ability and wonderful leadership skills . . . just kidding), I was able to take that church from a Sunday attendance of 120 all the way back to 54. I felt like a failure.

To say these were some very dark days of ministry would be an understatement. I repented and asked the Lord's forgiveness for thinking I could plant a church or even be a pastor. If you looked up failure in the dictionary, my picture would have been a living illustration of church planting failure. I honestly wanted them to fire me, but all the people who didn't like me had left the church already. The 54 remaining members were the ones who were hanging in there with this struggling preacher.

A few years later, my daughter Shari would give me some great encouragement that I could have used in that trying time. One day I was in my van with my family when we were driving back from a vacation. As we passed our church building, my sweet little daughter Shari said, "The best pastor in all the world preaches there." Tonia and I smiled at each other, realizing that she may have been a little biased towards her daddy. But I was thankful for her love and encouragement all the same!

God must have known there would be many days when I would need to remember Shari's sweet words of encouragement.

One day during the season when I felt like such a failure, my chairman of the board of elders, Gary, called and said he and his wife Karol would like to stop by because they wanted to talk to me.

I told my wife Tonia, "If they say they're leaving too, then I am done. I can't do this anymore." If you have ever felt like a failure in your job, in your relationship, or in anything that is important to you, then you know what I meant. You know it's in those dark moments when we are faced with the choice of quitting, even though when we began, that was the last thing we had wanted to do.

When Gary and Karol arrived, we sat down in our living room where for the last three years, we had had several prayer meetings with them and others from our church. We had prayed together multiple times for our struggling little congregation. I was a little nervous as I tried to anticipate what Gary might say.

Gary looked at me and said, "We want you to know that we believe in you, and we will follow Christ and help build this church with you!"

Gary's words were like strength to my life. He and Karol believed in me when I didn't believe in myself. I think of them when I read Job 4:3–4: "Think how you have instructed many. How you have strengthened feeble hands. Your words have supported those who stumbled. You have strengthened faltering knees." In that season, my knees were buckling under the spiritual battle that was waging for this young congregation. But with Gary and Karol's support, I knew that if they were going with me, I could keep going. How could I quit?

Dream

During that same season, our church had scheduled a guest speaker, Dr. Waylon Moore, to do a conference on discipleship. Dr. Moore was a well-known leader and a sought-after speaker. I was almost ashamed of how little our church was and how much we were struggling. I knew he had spoken to crowds of thousands. We were fortunate to get 30–40 people for a weeknight service.

During one of the sessions, Dr. Moore was talking about Scripture memorization. He said, "You need to attach any problem you might have to a promise in Scripture." As an example, he shared 1 Peter 5:7: "Cast your cares upon Him because He cares for you." He taught us to take a problem we have and give it to God because He cares for us.

Later that night I was walking back and forth in our living room, praying. I said, "God, I cast this church upon You because You care for Your church." I kept saying it over and over. With tears now flowing down my face, I prayed, "God, I cast Your church upon You."

Then I felt like the weight of the world lifted off my shoulders, and a peace beyond my understanding filled my heart. It was like the Holy Spirit was just waiting for me to let go and let God plant this church. In Matthew 16:18, Jesus said, "I will build my church and the gates of hell will not prevail against it." I needed to surrender to Jesus and let Him plant His church.

During this time, I would often journal and write out my prayers. I also would jot down my dreams if I felt they might have some spiritual meaning. In the Bible, God often used the avenue of dreams to reveal His direction. Now, I realize a dream could be from a bad meal, a bad movie, or a bad memory. But if I felt the dream had a spiritual meaning, I would write down the details of the dream and pray for insight.

One night I dreamed of being at our church service. When I stepped up to the pulpit to speak, I saw that the church was packed full of people with faces I did not recognize. Then I awoke. I said, "Oh Lord, this is what I pray for, and this is what I dream of." A couple of days later, I had another dream. I saw a new building with a new sanctuary, and when I got up to speak, it was again full of people I did not know. I awoke and prayed, "Oh Lord, this is what I pray for, and this is what I dream of."

A few days after I had those dreams, I was reading about Joseph in Genesis 41:25–33. This passage describes Joseph's interpretation of Pharaoh's dream. Joseph said to Pharaoh, "The dreams of Pharaoh are one and the same. God has revealed to Pharaoh what He is about to do. . . . The reason the dream was given to Pharaoh in two forms is that the matter has been firmly decided by God, and God will do it soon" (Genesis 41:25, 32).

My heart was warmed when I thought about my two dreams and how this Scripture passage related to my experience. My two dreams were alike. Could God be revealing what He had decided and was about to do soon? Could it be that the people He would call and lead would soon be coming to this floundering church plant?

Church Growth

At this time, I had an office at my home. In my office, I had a coat closet I used as my prayer closet. I was inspired to make this closet a special place for me to pray after reading Matthew 6:6: "Jesus said, 'When you pray, go into your room (closet), close the door and pray to your Father who is in heaven. Then your Father, who sees what is done in secret, will reward you.'"

So I took Jesus' words literally. I took a reading pillow, placed it on the floor, and I would crawl in and shut the door while I prayed for my church and my family. The closet had a light with a pull string I could turn on while I read the Scriptures or journaled. To say I loved the prayer closet would be an understatement. It was like I was hiding away with God, and I shared with Him my deepest struggles.

When my daughters were little, they would come back to my office. When they noticed I wasn't at my desk, they knew I was in the prayer closet. They would come over to the door, knock, and quietly say, "Daddy, can I pray with you?"

I would open the door, and they would climb in and sit on my lap. I'd say, "Okay, you pray first, and then I'll pray for you." They didn't stay long, but they all joined me in the prayer closet at one point or another. Our children grew up knowing prayer was important to Mom and Dad. (Tonia and I ended up having five children in all, with our daughter Mary being born in 1987 and our son David being born in 1991.)

Each night I would also pray with our children as we put them to bed. Our oldest daughter Sara was eight at the time. I said to her, "Honey, let's pray and ask God to bring one new family a month to our church." I was thinking if an average family had four people, and we gained twelve new families over the next year, it would almost double the size of the church. (Remember, I had taken the church from 120 people back to 54.)

Sara said, "Dad, you can pray for one a month if you want to, but I am going to pray for one a week."

I said, "Honey, you go right ahead. All the faith I have right now is for one a month."

There was probably a smile in the prayer court of heaven that night, thinking let this little child lead the pastor. That next Sunday we had our first new family. Sara was all smiles. One for Sara and zero for Dad since I was believing for only one a month. The next week another new family showed up—two for Sara. For the next twelve weeks, we had another new family join us each week. God heard the prayer of my young daughter and answered her childlike faith!

I think the biggest miracle was not only that these families visited, but that they stayed and helped plant the church. I kept track of the new families coming and noticed we had twenty-six new families join us over a twenty-six-week period. Just as in Genesis 42, God fulfilled the two dreams He had given me: "The matter has been firmly decided by God, and God will do it soon" (Genesis 42:32).

The new sanctuary I saw in my dream—we actually built it. This sanctuary was built at a new location about seven miles from the Seventh-day Adventist church we had been leasing for almost five years. At that point, we renamed the church Brookville Road Community Church to identify with our new location.

The property for Brookville Road Community Church was across the street from a beautiful housing development with expensive homes. A member of our church at the time said, "People living in those homes will never come to hear a pig farmer preach." She was right. Not many would come to hear a pig farmer, but many would come to hear Jesus speak through one who was surrendered to the Holy Spirit's leading. God is able to take all of us from humble beginnings to do His good works. I'm not sure what your pig pen looks

like or what your pulpit will be. But God does. The field is
ripe for the harvest, and the Lord is looking for laborers. Will
you be one?

Promises to Read:

Luke 4:18: "The Spirit of the Lord is on me, because He
has anointed me to proclaim good news to the poor. He has
sent me to proclaim freedom for the prisoners and recovery
of sight for the blind to set the oppressed free."

Luke 10:2: "The harvest is plentiful, but the workers are
few. Ask the Lord of the harvest, therefore, to send out
workers into his harvest field."

1 Corinthians 1:26–27, 31: "Brothers and sisters, think
of what you were when you were called. Not many of you
were wise by human standards; not many were influential;
not many were of noble birth. But God chose the foolish
things of the world to shame the wise; God chose the weak
things of the world to shame the strong . . . Therefore, as it
is written: 'Let the one who boasts boast in the Lord.'"

Ephesians 2:10: "For we are God's handiwork, created
in Christ Jesus to do good works, which God prepared in
advance for us to do."

Prayer to Pray:

Lord, if it's true You are looking for workers, I want to sign up so that You might use my life. Take my life and glorify our heavenly Father with it. In Jesus' name I pray, Amen!

3

Small Steps with God

Often people ask me, "How do you have faith to raise money for a ministry?" Admittedly, raising enough funds to pay salaries, cover operating expenses, and maintain a ministry can be a daunting task. Sometimes this pressure can consume my mind. But the reason I trust God to meet our needs in miraculous ways now, at the age of sixty-six, is because I have chosen to take steps of faith to trust God in each season of my life as I walked with Him. I couldn't be the leader I am today if I hadn't walked the journey of trusting God back when I was in my twenties, thirties, forties, and fifties. In this chapter, I will share some of the small faith steps I took, trusting God to meet our needs. I'm not sure what your small steps of faith will look like in your life, but I hope the illustrations from my life will encourage you to step out in faith and walk with the Lord.

I have learned the truth of Hebrews 11:6: "Without faith it is impossible to please God, because anyone who comes to Him must believe He exists and that He rewards those who earnestly seek Him." But this doesn't mean I haven't found myself in many overwhelming situations. Honestly, I have never felt that I had the gift of faith. My faith for others has always been greater than my faith for my own needs. It was easy to believe God would answer prayers for others, but when it was a prayer that I prayed for my own needs, doubt would creep in. Maybe you are the same way. Maybe you have thought, *Why would God do this for me?*

I love Jesus' words in Matthew 17:20: "I tell you, if you have faith as small as a mustard seed, you can say to this mountain, move from here to there and it will move. Nothing will be impossible for you." Mustard seeds are usually about one to two millimeters in diameter. They are often referred to as grains, like grains of sand. Mustard seeds are so small that they are hardly seen or noticed. I have often said, "Sure, I have a grain of faith. My faith is small, but small faith can do big things!"

Through the many years and challenges, I can't tell you how many times I have failed to trust the promises God has given. But in the school of faith, I didn't give up. I just kept getting up and looking up for more grace. There are days for me, and maybe for you too, on which a little faith is all I have. When the mountain is in your way, and it seems immovable, what do you do? I have faced large mountains in my life—trying to meet my children's needs as I juggled ministry, farming, and family life. I have faced the mountain of walking myself and my loved ones through grief as we endured heart-wrenching tragedies. I have climbed the mountain of criticism and persecution in my leadership. At times, I have been overwhelmed at the mountain of financial loss when investments didn't work out . . . the list could go on and on.

What mountains have you faced in your life? When you are faced with an overwhelming problem, how do you respond?

Once, when I was facing what seemed to me a large mountain, my good friend, Pastor Greg said to me, "That's no mountain for a mountain climber."

I so appreciated his words. If the mountains aren't moved, let's climb them, so we can get a better look at what God is doing! Hebrews 11:1 says, "Now faith is confidence in what we hope for and assurance about what we do not see." I have always prayed for eyes of faith—20/20 vision to see the unseen.

George Mueller's Faith

One of the books I read early in my Christian life was *George Mueller: He Dared to Trust God for the Needs of Countless Orphans* by Faith Coxe Bailey. Even though I read this book over forty years ago, I still remember the impact that George Mueller's faith had on me.

But before George Mueller started any ministry that would end up impacting thousands of orphans, he had an encounter with God. At the age of 20, George Mueller prayed this prayer: "At last! God, tonight I am Yours." He stayed there on his knees for almost half an hour. Then he got up and sat down on his bed. He knew something wonderful had happened to him!"[i]

This prayer of surrender must be part of why George Mueller became such a great man of faith. In 1836, Mueller's faith compelled him and his wife to start five orphan homes in Bristol, England, and his ministry cared for over 10,000 orphaned children before Mueller's death. George did not receive any government funding, but he believed in faith that God would provide for the children's needs. During his lifetime, George's orphan homes received over 1.5 million pounds, which would be worth over 117 million U.S. dollars in today's currency.

George's story caused me to look up and believe God for greater things. I marveled that George's faith impacted a whole generation in England. I have always wanted to serve

God and give my life for a worthy cause of helping others come to know Christ. Reading about George's life and ministry showed me that he had taken steps of faith in his journey of serving Christ.

I am not a theologian (did I hear some "Amens!" and "That's obvious!"?), and I am not trying to do a thesis on faith. I want to share some basic, elementary truths I have learned by walking with God for forty-six years. I want to tell you how God has challenged me to exercise my faith and trust Him. Examples like George Mueller have taught me to trust God and take steps toward a faith-filled future.

Steps of Faith

As I mentioned in the previous chapter, Tonia and I took our first step of faith as a couple in 1977 when I quit my job, and we left the farm to go to Bible college in Kansas. We believed that God would provide for us somehow. As you already know, during my second year of Bible college, I was hired by the host church of the Bible college as a quarter-time youth pastor. My salary was $250 a month. As a young couple with two young daughters, we were completely dependent on God's care for us. The $250 monthly salary didn't seem like much to others, but God continued to provide for us with scholarships, part-time jobs, income from my farm, and even gifts in the mail. To my surprise, I graduated without any college debt, which to me was God showing His gracious hand of provision.

During my first year as a youth pastor, a wonderful Christian lady, Lucille Jacks, who was heading up our Christian education committee at church, said to me, "Youth want to do something active, so come up with a project that the church can get behind."

Taking her advice, I decided I would take our Sr. High Youth Group on a mission trip to Haiti. I researched where we could go in Haiti and how much the trip would cost. There were thirteen high school students in our church youth group. I went to these students and asked, "How many of you want to go to Haiti on a mission trip?"

All thirteen hands went up.

So I said, "Okay, we need to get busy and do some fundraisers."

I needed to raise $9,000 in 1978. Using the inflation calculator, this would be around $40,900 in 2022.

At the first parents' meeting I held for the mission trip, I remember informing the parents that each student would have to raise $600. One student's mother asked me, "What are you going to do when a youth falls short of the $600? They will still want to go, even if they can't raise all the money."

I said to this concerned mom, "I am not going to have that problem," and went right to the next question.

After I had answered all the questions, this mom said, "Really, what will you do if a young person has only $300 of the $600 needed?"

I looked at her and said, "I can't even think that way because if these kids think I am doubting, they will too! I must believe we can raise this money."

We prayed for God to move and bless in unexpected ways—and He did!—but we also rolled up our sleeves and went to work! We did all kinds of projects and fundraisers to help earn money. We did bake sales, garage sales, benefit basketball games, etc. It was during all these service projects and the time we spent working together that I got to know these young people, and they got to know me. This was the breakthrough in my ministry I was looking for. For one of our fundraisers, we made 500 pizzas and sold them for four dollars each. I remember how excited we were when one of the teenage guys returned from delivering a pizza. A college couple had given him fifty dollars and told him to use it toward our trip!

Through all these efforts, God raised all the money for our trip in forty days. In the Bible, the time period of forty days or years is a time of testing. The nation of Israel spent forty years wandering in the wilderness. Jesus spent forty days fasting and being tempted by Satan in the desert. I believe this forty days of raising the funds for the Haiti trip was a test of my faith, as well.

After the Sunday morning service, when we celebrated the goal having been accomplished, the mom who had asked me what I was going to do when a youth failed to come up with the money came up to me. She said, "I was saving money, and I didn't get to give it, so what shall I do?" She was now surprised that all the money had been raised, and her face showed that she was feeling left out. This confirmed to me that everyone needs to be part of a blessing!

I said to her, "Give the money you have saved—that way if unexpected expenses come up, we will have money to cover them." I think all of us—the church community, the youth group, and this young youth pastor—learned a lot about faith that year.

Trusting God to Provide for My Family

In 1986, Tonia and I needed to take another step of faith when we were three years into our church plant. As you may recall, church attendance had gone from one hundred and twenty members back to fifty-four. Because of this, the church could not afford to pay me. As a church, we had been saving to buy land, and now the church would need to start taking money out of the land fund to pay my salary. I really didn't want that to happen, so I felt like the Lord said to me, "Trust me and live by faith!"

So on a Sunday morning, I said to the congregation, "I feel God wants me to live by faith, trust Him, and not receive a salary for a while. I know you want to provide for your pastor but let me do this in obedience to the Lord!"

I remember a month went by, and my mortgage and car payment were due. Tonia and I had three children at that point, and I was not sure what God was going to do to provide for our family. One day I went to my mailbox, and inside it was an envelope. There was no name written on it—it was just a blank envelope. I opened it, and inside was some cash! First, I saw some fifty-dollar bills, so I counted: 1, 2, 3, 4, 5, 6, 7, 8. Then I counted the one-hundred-dollar bills—1, 2, 3, 4. The total was eight hundred dollars—enough to pay my mortgage and car payment!

This young, floundering church plant started to rally around this step of faith. It was like the congregation thought, "Wow, this young pastor is serious about planting this church. Let's help him."

The church members started bringing my family all kinds of food. They brought us grocery bags full of food, including frozen meat for us to stock our freezer. Finally, after we had received so much of their generous gifts of food, one Sunday I stood and told our congregation, "My wife asked me to share with you to please not bring us any more food for a while. Our cupboards and freezer have never been so full!"

I know this was a joy for them to hear me say—that God had supplied enough already. We started to feel their love and support. They received me as their pastor, and I loved them as their shepherd. During this time of living by faith, I was taking baby steps toward trusting God for a faith-filled future.

Living the Walk

After our congregation purchased the land on which to build Brookville Road Community Church, I took my two oldest daughters, Sara (age 8) and Rachel (age 6), to go see the property. On the property there is an old oak tree—over 330 years old. We were standing under this beautiful tree, and I asked the girls, "Can you see God's church?"

They said, "No."

I told them, "I can."

They said, "You can?"

"Yep!"

They asked, "Where is it? We don't see anything but soybeans." (In Indiana, corn and soybeans are the primary crops for farmers.)

I said, "You have to see it with eyes of faith. I can see it by faith." I pointed again to the land where the church building would be built and asked them, "Can you see it now?"

They looked up at me with wide, questioning eyes and nodded.

Later the girls asked each other if they had seen anything. They both confessed, "No, I was just agreeing with Dad."

One asked, "Do you think Dad actually saw God's church?"

The other said, "I am not sure. He said he did!"

I remember looking out across that soybean field, visualizing the building, and hoping it would soon be a reality. I was seeing the unseen—using my mustard seed faith, just a small grain of faith, to believe God would build His church. I was applying apostle Paul's words in 2 Corinthians 5:7: "For we walk by faith, not by sight."

What does it mean for us to walk with God? This is beautifully demonstrated by one of my favorite men in the Old Testament, Enoch, who lived prior to Noah's flood. Genesis 5:21–23 says, "When Enoch lived sixty-five years, he became the father of Methuselah. Enoch walked faithfully with God for three hundred years and had other sons and daughters. Altogether Enoch lived a total of three hundred sixty-five years." In Genesis 5:24, we see the significance of Enoch walking with God again: "And Enoch walked with God and he was not, for God took him." The author of Hebrews in the New Testament gives us some more insight about Enoch in Hebrews 11:5–6: "By faith Enoch was taken from this life, so that he did not experience death. He could not be found, because God had taken him away. For before he was taken, he was commended as one who pleased God. And without faith it is impossible to please God."

Yet there is something unique and humble about Enoch. We know he was a preacher of righteousness, but to our knowledge, he never performed one miracle, never planted a church or grew a church to be a megachurch, never founded a movement or caused a great revival. All we know for sure is that he walked with God and did it quite well.

When I think about my life, I often think about all the things I have not done that I wish I could have done for God. But Enoch did not feel that way. All Enoch needed and wanted was to walk with his God. He so pleased God that God took him to be with Him before his death. This example has helped me realize that it is not what I do for our Lord that pleases Him, though I know my obedience does. It is my simple faith, my personal, daily walk with Him that pleases the Lord. I have realized that the most important thing I can do is learn how to walk with God to develop a personal relationship with Him and be aware of His presence every day.

Every day we are bombarded with all kinds of distractions that keep us from focusing on just walking well with God. Charles R. Swindoll once wrote, "Our great tendency in this age is to increase our speed, to run faster, even in Christian life. In the process our walk with God stays shallow, and our tank runs low on fumes. Intimacy offers a full tank of fuel that can only be found by pulling up closer to God, which requires taking necessary time and going to the effort to make that happen." Often the fast pace of life distracts us.

Could it be that the most important thing about walking with God is just taking the time to do so? My wife and I live back on the same farm I purchased in 1975, and our lane is one-third of a mile long. (Since I moved back to Indiana in 1983, in addition to pastoring, I have partnered with my younger brother J.R. to keep farming soybeans and corn.) Tonia and I enjoy taking walks on our farm. We both know how to walk. On our walks we pray, talk, and enjoy each other's presence. The only thing that keeps us from our walks is just taking the time. Dillon Burroughs writes about the simplicity of pleasing God: "There is no secret formula, only a life committed to a close walk with God." We need to keep it simple. The more complicated we make our walk, the more we feel we must learn, know, or apply the right formula, and the less likely we will be free to walk with God.

I doubt if Enoch got up every day and asked himself, "What formula do I use to walk with God today?"

No, I think he got up and rejoiced in the day and set out for a good walk with God. It has been said that one day on their walk, God said to Enoch, "We are closer to my house than yours, so come on home with me." And Enoch did.

I have been walking with God now for forty-six years, and my walk has gotten so much better as the years have passed. I have become a worshiper, a lover of God, and now know what it means to delight in Him. One day in the future on my walk with Jesus, He will say to me, "I have been preparing a place for you. Come with me and see it." I can't wait! But until then, I will just keep walking.

As I have shared, I started taking little steps of faith: Trusting God to provide for our Haiti youth mission trip, trusting God while my family and I were living by faith for our mortgage and car payments, and then in 1986, having a mustard-seed faith while praying and seeing the church building with eyes of faith. These were all small steps toward walking with God. Like a toddler, I was putting one foot in front of the other. Slowly a toddler learns to walk, and slowly I learned to put one step of faith in front of the other. Today Brookville Road Community Church has a 15-acre campus and 80,000 square feet facility as they continue to step out and trust God. The old oak tree still stands today and is a towering reminder of an earlier day when a pastor and his young daughters saw God's church before she even existed. For we walk by faith and not by sight! I'm not sure if you are facing a mountain or even something greater, but let me say: Take a step of faith. Trust God to do something in and through your life. Try with the eyes of faith to visualize your goal or your dream and start taking steps toward it. Step out in faith and just keep walking. Enjoy your adventure with God.

Promises to Read

Hebrews 11:6: "Without faith it is impossible to please God, because anyone who comes to Him must believe He exists and that He rewards those who earnestly seek Him."

Micah 6:8: "He has shown you, O mortal, what is good. And what does the LORD require of you? To act justly and to love mercy and to walk humbly with your God."

Read these quotes and let them sink deep into your heart. "Most of all, God has blessed us by giving us the privilege of knowing Him and walking with Him every day. He did this by sending His Son into the world to die for our sins."

—Billy Graham

"Smart men walked on the moon. Daring men walked on the ocean floor, but wise men walk with God." — Leonard Ravenhill

---

Prayer to Pray

Father, help me to learn to walk with you daily as I step out by faith. Increase my faith when I doubt. Help me to realize that all things are possible with you. In Jesus' name, Amen!

Oak tree outside of Brookville Road Community Church

4

A Taste of Revival

I have a file in my office desk titled "Revival Preaching." Inside are messages I have preached on revival over the forty-six years of my time in ministry. I've kept these messages because I've always wanted to see God do more. In my heart, I've always known the Holy Spirit wanted to do more in the lives of His people.

So many people are discouraged in life because they listen to themselves: to all the negative thoughts that flow through our minds each day. The psalmist says to stop listening to yourself and start preaching to yourself! Have you ever preached to yourself? Boy, I have! I have said, "Hey, my soul, why are you downcast? O my soul, why are you so disturbed within me? Put your hope in God—for I will praise Him, my Savior and my God! Fight for hope, soul. Look up instead of looking at yourself! Soul, you need renewal, you need a taste of revival!"

When I was in Bible college in 1981, I had a class in homiletics, which is the art of preaching or writing sermons. During the semester, all pastoral students had to prepare and deliver a message during the weekly student body chapel. This weekly service was held in Philips Hall, and about 200 students and college staff attended. Chapel started at 11:30 a.m. and would finish quickly when the town whistle blew, letting everyone know it was noon and lunchtime. Many of the college students looked forward to lunch because most skipped breakfast.

For whatever reason, as I began preparing my message for this assignment, I chose to preach on the topic, "What will prayer and fasting do?" In the church I attended when I got saved, a man named John encouraged me to pray and fast for God's leading in my life. From the very beginning of my new life in Christ, prayer and fasting have been spiritual disciplines I have practiced. Since I was speaking on prayer and fasting, I thought I should fast for several days before my big moment.

My sermon text was Acts 13:1–4: "Now there were at Antioch, in the church that was there, prophets and teachers, Barnabas, and Simeon who was called Niger, and Lucius of

Cyrene and Manaen who had been brought up with Herod the tetrarch and Saul. While they were ministering to the Lord and fasting, the Holy Spirit said, 'Set apart for Me Barnabas and Saul for the work to which I have called them.' Then when they had fasted and prayed and laid their hands on them, they sent them away. So, being sent out by the Holy Spirit, they went down to Seleucia, and from there they sailed to Cyrus."

My sermon's focus was, "What will prayer and fasting do?" That morning I proclaimed, "It will send us out with the call of God and with the anointing of the Holy Spirit. It will put us in a position to discern God's direction for our lives." I challenged the student body to seek God's will and direction for their lives. I spoke passionately, and when I finished, I sat down. All was still and quiet for a few moments. Then some students got out of their seats, started to come forward, and knelt at the front of the chapel.

Students were praying and ministering to each other. Then, one at a time, students stood to testify to what had just happened in their hearts or how they were challenged by God's word. The noon whistle blew, signaling that chapel was over and lunch would be served, but the dean of students didn't come forward to dismiss and close in prayer. The students kept sharing. There were tears, confessions, and praises for what our Lord was doing. It was like a divine moment when God showed up and showered love on His people. The college kitchen staff were wondering, *Where are the students? How long can we keep the food warm?* The faculty then canceled all afternoon classes and sent us out to enjoy the afterglow of these wonderful moments.

I don't know all that God did in the hearts of the students, but I do know that my prayer and fasting had put me in a position to receive God's direction for my life. He opened a door that day for me to become the youth pastor at the host church for the Bible college, where I would spend the next five years serving and learning. That chapel service was a little taste of revival for all of us, some manna coming down from heaven to feed our hungry souls. No lunch was needed.

Something Missing?

Do you long for a chapel moment like that? Do you ever hunger for more of God's presence in your life and in your church? Most people see their church as doing just fine— maybe it boasts of wonderful people, good fellowship, beautiful facilities, great coffee, uplifting worship, anointed preaching, great coffee . . . (Oh, did I already mention *great coffee*? You can tell I enjoy a good cup of coffee.) Maybe the greeters are all saying the right things. Maybe there are good children's programs, youth programs, and small groups. Looking around the church, maybe it looks great and is growing, but deep down in your heart, you know something is missing. You are longing for more. There is an internal hunger, a thirst, a desire that will not allow you to go through the motions of your Christian life. You're not satisfied with the way it is.

Could I say, "Good for you!"? I wouldn't want it any other way! God wouldn't want it any other way. My prayer for you is that you will long, thirst, and hunger for more of God. As Jesus said in Matthew 5:6, "Blessed are those who hunger and thirst for righteousness for they shall be filled." My prayer is that you will always be praying, hoping, and becoming a lifelong seeker of Him.

One day, sometime in the 1990s, while at my church office, I received this note from a dear brother in the Lord:

> "As you said on Sunday, God is wanting to use our church in a mighty way as in a revival. I sense that also, and look expectantly as to how he will bring it about. I want to be part of it too. My heart has been changed every year I have been here at the church. I want to thank you for being faithful in preaching the word and challenging me to strive for the best God has for me. Your brother in Christ, Bill."

I love Bill's heart—"I want to be part of it too!"

Yet some of us are more than satisfied with how church is today. Life pushes us to be satisfied, to sit down and be comfortable. Life rocks us to sleep and causes us to become complacent and think all is well. We are much like my grandfather's pocket watch that I had to hand wind, so it wouldn't run down and stop keeping time. Our Christian life can just run down. We lose our spiritual desire. We become less willing to attempt the difficult, the daring, or even the dangerous for God. Before we know it, we let down our guard and begin to drift along, thinking our Christian life is something we do on Sunday. May God help us if this is our life!

In 1999 we did a twelve-week study called *Experiencing God* by Henry T. Blackaby and Claude V. King as a church. The study was about knowing and doing the will of God. (I might say up front that this is an excellent study if you have never done it.) I have gone through it three times now, and I keep learning new truths. One time I wrote these thoughts in my journal: "One day at a time—live today in God's will—seeking first His kingdom (Matt 6:33). Lord, help me to seek your kingdom first every day, not weekly or monthly or yearly, but daily. Lord, let me live your will today."

As part of my sermon preparation, I would leave my church office for a quieter place. A couple in our church had an in-law apartment attached to their home, and I would go there to study and worship. On this study day, I was working through the *Experiencing God* study. All of a sudden, it was like the finger of God touched my heart. I can't describe it. I just knew God was present, and I had just experienced God in a brand-new way. Something good had happened—even though I didn't know what. For whatever reason, I felt prompted to leave the couple a note on the desk before I left. I wrote, "I want you to know God touched my heart today."

When I left, I headed to lunch at a local restaurant. While I was eating, the Holy Spirit whispered these words: *Revival is going to break out at the church on Sunday.* The impression of this message was so overwhelming that I started to cry at my table. After a while, my waitress asked me if I was alright.

I answered, "Yes. I am so blessed."

Because of my tears, she said, "I wish I could believe you."

After our brief conversation, I just sat there, taking in the wonderful news. I was thinking, *If revival is going to break out at the church on Sunday, I'd better prepare. I will start fasting—but not until I have dessert.* I left the restaurant with a full stomach, a heart ready to pray, and faith that the Holy Spirit's message would come true.

It is hard to explain how I felt—filled with anticipation, yet nervous about how this would happen. If revival was coming, I would not need the message I had prepared for Sunday. Surely, God had something else He wanted to share.

I think some of you reading this chapter have prayed for revival or heard others pray for revival. You may have, at one time or another in your spiritual journey, been present when a revival shower came, even if it was for a brief moment. It could have been during a worship meeting, at a

Bible conference, or during your quiet time when God's gracious Spirit of love and goodness washed over you like a refreshing shower, leaving you feeling clean and filling you with a new desire to draw closer to God.

Faith and Doubt

If you have been part of a service when the Holy Spirit has taken over and people have become real and transparent, you will long for another moment like that. I long for these moments. I pray and fast for these kinds of moments. So when the Holy Spirit said, *Revival is going to break out at the church on Sunday*, you can imagine my excitement.

As I was driving home, the Holy Spirit whispered to me, "Stop at this house and tell them that revival is going to break out at church on Sunday." This couple had been a big part of our church but had experienced some disappointing circumstances, and they had stopped attending. Instead of obeying, I drove right on by. I thought, *That was just me thinking that*. But then the Holy Spirit said, *Go back and tell them*.

So I turned my car around, drove back, and parked in their driveway. I got out, walked up to this home I had been to on many occasions, and knocked on the front door. The wife answered the door and welcomed me, "Hi, Pastor, what brings you by?"

I got straight to the point. "The Holy Spirit told me to stop and let you know that revival is going to break out at the church on Sunday."

She must have been shocked by my words because she just looked at me. It appeared to me that her husband had been hiding behind the door, but he must have heard my confession too. He stepped out, looked at me, and said, "Pastor, we will be there."

"That sounds great. See you Sunday."

As I turned to walk to my car, the spiritual battle between faith and doubt began. My mind began questioning, *Do I believe what God has said, or is it nothing more than wishful thinking? Did God by His Holy Spirit really say that, or did I just think it up?* Over the next four days, I experienced the most intense spiritual warfare I had ever faced until that point.

The next day I turned the church's sanctuary into my personal prayer center and invited my prayer partners to come and join me. I knew I had to confess to everyone what was going to take place on Sunday.

During this time of prayer and seeking, I was led to read several books on revival. I specifically felt led to reread *One Divine Moment: The Account of the Asbury Revival of 1970* written by Robert E. Coleman and David J. Gyertson. As I read, I felt the Holy Spirit give me His plan: "What I want you to do on Sunday is get up, and instead of preaching, I want you to read several of these testimonies from *One Divine Moment.* After you read these stories, I will do it again." My heart rejoiced as I felt assurance that God was leading and wanting to bring revival.

As people began to hear revival was coming, they started showing up in the sanctuary to pray. People were praying and longing for God to move through our church.

Finally, Sunday morning came. I was up early and at the church by 6 a.m. In my office, I was under so much spiritual warfare that tears were running down my cheeks and dripping onto my chair mat. It sounded like a leak in the roof. You could hear the tears drop, one at a time, and hit the mat by my feet. I am ashamed to admit it, but I was thinking: *Oh my, what if God doesn't do this? What if I didn't hear correctly? If God doesn't come through, it could ruin my credibility and the integrity I have built over seventeen years of ministry at the church.*

Doubt is always lurking around faith, always trying to steal away our trust in what God has said. A church elder opened my office door. I lifted my face from my hands. He saw the tears wetting my cheeks, paused a moment, and then said, "You alright?"

I had heard these same words before—at the restaurant from the waitress! This gave me a sense of comfort that God was really going to do this.

"Yes," I said. "Just praying, trusting God will do what He said."

The Holy Spirit Wave

Our first service started at 9:00 a.m. We had chosen three songs. Then I was going to get up and start reading the testimonies from the Asbury Revival.

When it was my time to share, I stood and gave some opening comments about revival and introduced the book, *One Divine Moment*. Then, for the next ten minutes or so, I read testimonies from those present at the Asbury Revival in 1970.

Psalm 42:7 says, "Deep calls to deep in the roar of your waterfalls; all Your waves and breakers have swept over me." As I read one of the stories, I felt something sweep over me like a wave. I literally stepped back and stopped reading for a moment, not really sure of what had just happened or if others in the congregation had felt the same thing. When I had finished, I opened the altar for anyone to come and pray.

I sat on the steps, and my family all came and gathered around, praying. My youngest daughter, Mary, age eleven, looked up at me and said, "Daddy, I want a heart like yours!" Still today, this is the greatest compliment I have ever received—and it was from someone who lived with me every day. We prayed that God would do that for her. Today Mary is the associate director of Hope Center Indy. Her journey into ministry started at the age of four when she accepted Christ as her Savior and was confirmed on this day when we prayed for her to have her father's heart, the heart her heavenly Father had given her father.

The altar area filled up, and people even filled the aisles. People were crying and praying. Even those sitting in their seats were moved by what had just happened. The time for the first service to be over had come and gone. The people arriving for the second service were waiting in the foyer. So I stood and said, "If you want to stay, please do, but we are going to open the doors and let in our second-service people."

Many people continued to pray around the altar. The service team huddled for the 11:00 a.m. service. I told the worship team, "Let's do the same thing and see what God does."

I did the very same thing, reading from *One Divine Moment,* and at the end, God provided the same results. People flooded the altar area. We set up a microphone, and people lined up to share. People felt clean—like they had been washed by the Holy Spirit. My nephew testified that sitting there in his seat that day, he believed and was saved as the Holy Spirit washed over him. Our service usually ended around 12:00 noon, and now it was 1:30 p.m. I said, "Let's do this: Go home, get some lunch, and we will come back at 6:00 p.m. and see what God has in store."

For some, the anointing of the services had been so strong, it was like drinking from a fire hydrant. Instead of enjoying a cool drink of water, it splashed off, leaving them wondering what had just taken place. But for others, it was a moment they had prayed for, waited for, and now were living firsthand.

We came back that evening. After singing a few songs, we put a mic on a stand and invited people to share. As people shared, others came to the altar. Couples struggling with their marriage and others fighting battles all alone now had prayer support. My heart rejoiced in the openness, honesty, and confession of those who spoke. It was getting close to 9 p.m., so I said, "Let's go home and come back tomorrow night at 7:00 p.m. and see what God will do."

On Monday morning, I came to the church office. I was so grateful for Sunday and all that God was doing. I was still fasting (it was day five), so I said, "Lord, how long do you want me to fast?"

I heard Him tell me, *Forty days.*

Fear gripped my heart. The only people I knew of who had fasted for forty days were Moses, Elijah, and Jesus. I am not in their league. But I said, "Lord, if you help me, I will try."

I googled "fasting" and came across an article by Bill Bright, founder of Campus Crusade for Christ.

In his article, he shared how he was praying for two million Christians to fast and pray for forty days. As I read this, I felt God say, *You are one of them.*

The revival continued for several more days. There is one particular evening that stands out in my memory. Before the service began, I walked into the room beside the sanctuary where our worship team was standing in a circle to go over the order of worship and to pray. When I walked in, I smelled the most beautiful fragrance of roses. I mentioned, "Ladies, who has the perfume that smells like roses?"

They all looked at me and said, "None of us."

I said, "No, wait. Surely one of you is wearing this beautiful rose perfume." Everyone could smell this most beautiful fragrance, yet no one was wearing any perfume.

I don't know why, but I said, "Then the Rose of Sharon must be standing in our midst."

We know from Matthew 18:20: "For where two or three gather in my name, there am I with them." Even though this is Jesus' promise, we very rarely believe it is true that our Savior is ever present and wants us to know He is with us.

There is an old hymn that refers to Jesus as the Rose of Sharon, and that is what helped us to make the connection between Christ's presence and the fragrance we smelled in the prayer room.

Lord Jesus, My sweet Rose of Sharon,

my Prophet, my Priest, and my King.

Sweet Rose of Sharon, Oh Glory!

It's heavenly odor with fragrance my soul doth perfume.

That night in our pre-service prayer, the Rose of Sharon perfumed our room and our souls with His beautiful aroma.

During the next several nights, we had people from other churches and the community come to the services. On Wednesday night, I asked Gary Wright, President and Founder of World Renewal International, to share. He had been a student at Asbury College in 1970 during the revival, so I asked him to share what it was like for him at that revival. After he shared, he opened the altar. A pastor and the elders from another local church had heard about showers of revival, and they were present. They went to the altar to pray.

One of the elders was Tim, a local farmer I knew, so I stood behind him and prayed for God's blessing on him and that God would do a good work in him. Little did I know at the time what God was doing. The following Sunday, Tim went to teach his Sunday school class at his church, and he told them his story—that he had gone to a revival on Wednesday night and actually got saved. He was so transformed that he just had to share it with them. After sharing with his class, two couples prayed to receive Christ. During their church's worship service, he went to the podium and told his story again. He shared that he had been an elder for over thirty years, but on Wednesday night he had been saved at a revival.

Revival Memories

As I look back now twenty years later, it is hard to remember all the things God did during the revival. We had fourteen days of unscheduled revival. Lives were touched and changed. Many felt the refreshing showers of revival. James 5:7 reminds us: "Be patient, therefore brothers, until the coming of the Lord. See how the farmer waits for the first fruits of the earth, being patient about it, until it receives the early and the late rains."

As a farmer, I realize the importance of the early spring rains to get the seed that has been planted up and growing. Yet, it is the late rains that produce the harvest, the grain. We often say, "Rain makes grain." The late rain fills the ear of corn, the pods of soybeans, or the heads of wheat.

As a church, I felt we had had some early spring showers of revival, but the later rains are when a great harvest is produced. Let all of us keep longing and praying for the later rains and waves of the Holy Spirit.

Just as the Holy Spirit said, "Revival is going to break out at church on Sunday" at the restaurant that day, it surely did. From the moment in the study apartment when God touched my heart, a revival began, leading me into forty days of prayer and fasting, taking me deeper into a love relationship with Him, becoming a worshiper and intercessor. The person who got a revival in 1999 was this pastor, and I'm so glad I did! This is so true. The one who needs revival most is us. You might have heard of the story of drawing a circle on the floor and then stepping into the circle and praying, "God, bring revival, and please start in this circle!" When I stepped inside my personal circle, my revival began. I want you to know the Holy Spirit washed over me, changed me, and I have not been the same since.

I hope this chapter causes you to want more of God, pray for personal revival and church revival, and pray for the early and late rains that will bring a great harvest!

Promises to Read:

Psalm 42:1–2: "As the deer pants for streams of water, so my soul pants for you, my God. My soul thirsts for God, for the living God. When can I go and meet with God?"

Psalm 85:6: "Will you not revive us again, that your people may rejoice in you?"

Acts 3:19: "Repent, then, and turn to God, so that your sins may be wiped out, that times of refreshing may come from the Lord."

Prayer to Pray:

Lord, how I long for a closer relationship with You! Lead me down a path of personal revival, so my life can be changed and never be the same. In Jesus' name, Amen!

5

Launching Hope Center Indy

In 2015, I was sitting in the Upper Room at our church, which is a room we often used for prayer, when I opened my iPad to the L.A. Dream Center's website. When I was at a pastors' conference in Oklahoma City in the mid-1990s, I heard Pastor Tommy Barnett cast the vision about the first Dream Center in Los Angeles and tell the story of his son Matthew going to L.A. to start the ministry. The Dream Center is a Christian organization that works to "provide opportunities for people to rebuild and transform their lives... [by offering] the tools, education, and support through various programs available, all free of charge." [ii] The mission of the Dream Center stirred my heart as it truly was the church reaching out to the lost and hurting who need Christ. Through the years, I had made an effort to get updates on the ministry and read books by Tommy Barnett, including his book *Dream Again: Miracles Happen Every Day*. This book inspired me to think bigger for what God could do through my church in my city. As I saw how the Dream Center was showing the love of Christ to the people of L.A., I prayed that God would let me be part of a church that impacted its city like that!

On that day in 2015, I was browsing through the Dream Center's website when I came across a promotional video of a young woman who had experienced abuse and was caught in addiction. She felt she had no options left to escape the pain and addiction, and she tried to commit suicide. She explained that her last resort was going into a residential ministry at the L.A. Dream Center. Then she described how she had met Christ and, with the support of the Dream Center, was walking the path of healing and starting to build a new life for herself.

As I watched this video, I began to cry. I felt God breaking my heart for people in situations like this because it also broke God's heart to see them trapped in that cycle of pain. God was using this video to remind me of my desire to do something for the hurting in my city. I knew God was telling me that it was now or never. I was fifty-nine years old at that time, and if I was going to have the energy to start a new ministry, I would need to do it now.

Would I have the courage to step aside from the security of my position as a pastor and try to start something new? Was God really leading me to step aside from the church I had pastored for thirty-three years and step out by faith to start a ministry like the Dream Center?

My First Promise from God's Word

As a pastor, I write my sermon notes alongside passages in the Bible, so I get a new Bible every few years. About twenty-five years ago, I began to write in the front of each new Bible a message to myself. That message was this: "Go on, Hubert Nolen! Go on! Believe these promises!"

One Bible teacher said that he believes there are over forty thousand promises of God in the word. That means there are about 110 promises you can claim for each day of the year. That's a lot of promises you can stand upon, claim, receive, and believe!

About three months after I gave my life to Christ at the age of twenty, I received the first promise from God's word that I have ever received. As I mentioned in chapter 2, it was Luke 4:18: "The Spirit of the Lord is on me, because he has anointed me to proclaim good news to the poor. He has sent me to proclaim freedom for the prisoners and recovery of sight for the blind, to set the oppressed free." I remember the

Holy Spirit bore witness with my spirit when I received that word. I thought, *God is not only giving me this promise, God is calling me to be a preacher of the gospel of Jesus Christ.* For the last forty-six years, that promise has been fulfilled through my calling.

Have you ever received a promise from God's word? As you have read a verse of Scripture, did the Holy Spirit bear witness with your spirit, that this verse was really for you? But in those moments, have you asked, "God, are You really saying this to me? How will You actually accomplish this promise through me in this day that I live?"

I want to share with you about a promise that God gave to me in 2006 that I believe was meant for the Hope Center. That promise is Haggai 2:18–19: "From this day on, from this twenty-fourth day of the ninth month, give careful thought to the day when the foundation of the Lord's temple was laid. Give careful thought: Is there yet any seed left in the barn? Until now, the vine and the fig tree, the pomegranate and the olive tree have not borne fruit. 'From this day on I will bless you.'"

The phrase I want you to grab out of that promise is "on the twenty-fourth day of the ninth month, from this day on, I will bless you."

Even if you are familiar with the Bible, this is probably not a verse you memorized as a child or even in your Bible studies as an adult. But God highlighted this verse to me, and I believe He gave it to me as a promise!

How Can You Know If a Promise Is for You?

Let me share with you some insight into how you can begin to know about the promises of God. There are four different kinds of promises in God's word.

1. **Limited Promises.** This means the promise was for someone specific in the Bible, like Abraham. God said to Abraham, "Abraham, you're going to have a son and his name will be Isaac. And through him all the nations will be blessed." This was a limited promise. It was given specifically to Abraham regarding his son.

    Then there are promises that God gave to the nation of Israel. I love how Joshua says in Joshua 21:45, "Not one of all the Lord's good promises to Israel failed; every one was fulfilled." In other words, there are limited promises given to individuals as well as to groups, such as the nation of Israel.

2. **General Promises.** The apostle Paul says in 2 Corinthians 1:20: "All the promises are yes and amen in Jesus." In other words, every promise that is general is for you. You can claim it. It is yes and amen in Jesus Christ because of what He has done for you--because of His life, death, and resurrection.

3. **Conditional Promises.** These are "if–then" promises. If you do this, then God will do his part. Romans 10:9: "If you confess with your mouth, 'Jesus is Lord,' and believe in your heart that God has raised him from the dead, you will be saved." You do your part by confessing and believing, and God does his part by saving.

4. **Unconditional Promises.** These have nothing to do with us whatsoever—aren't you glad? They have everything to do with God's power, His majesty, His glory. They have everything to do with God's will, His purpose, His kindness, His goodness. 2 Peter 3:13 states: "But in keeping with his promise we are looking forward to a new heaven and a new earth, where righteousness dwells." You and I are looking forward to that day when there will be a new heaven and a new earth. It has nothing to do with us. It has everything to do with our God.

The promises of God fall into one of these four categories: limited, general, conditional, and unconditional. But the question we're trying to answer is this: If you receive a promise from God, how do you know if it's for you? And how do you know how God is going to reveal that to you and accomplish it in your life?

I don't know for sure how you try to discern this, but I'll share what I do when I believe God has given me a promise from His word.

1. When I'm reading along in God's word, and I feel that God is saying to me by the witness of His Spirit, "This verse of Scripture right here is for you," then I write it down in my prayer journal.

2. I begin to pray over it. *God, how are you going to accomplish this in my life? What will this look like in my life? How are You going to do this in the day in which I live?*

3. I study the verse by doing a word study on every word in that verse and cross-referencing every word. I want to know everything about that verse and its related passages. I want to know how God is going to use it. I want to see every part of it. So I write it down, pray over it, study it, and hide the promise in my heart.

4. I keep revisiting it. Often what happens when you and I get a promise from God is that we think it's going to happen tomorrow. Or next week. Or next month. Surely, it won't happen years down the road. But often we need to wait on God's timing, and while we wait, we have to keep meditating on that promise and watching for it to be fulfilled.

Promise Given

In 2006, I got the promise from Haggai: "On the ninth month the 24th day, from this day forward I'm going to bless you." Every year when the ninth month and 24th day came, I revisited it and prayed, "Okay, God. How are you going to answer this? How are you going to bring this about?"

As time passes—even years—it's not easy to wait. But during this time of waiting, I believe we need to continue revisiting the promise God gave us. Then we wait to see what God will do because God will bring it about in His timing.

In 2006, He gave me this promise. The events that led up to God giving me this promise are important to share. Every year in January, our church would join together to do twenty-one days of prayer and fasting. These twenty-one days were our way to ask God to refresh us, renew us, anoint us, change us, and bless our church, families, and community. In 2006, many of our church staff expanded the commitment of twenty days of prayer and fasting by doing a forty-day fast. Many chose to do a liquid fast with me. Others decided to fast one meal a day, fast one day a week, fast from other specific foods such as sugar, or fast from any other significant thing that would be a sacrifice. During this time, we kept asking God to bless our members and their families and to do His will in their lives.

At the end of that forty-day fast that year, I felt like God said to me, "Don't stop."

I said, "Okay, I won't stop. But how long do you want me to keep fasting?" I began to think that maybe I should push on to fifty days because fifty is symbolic of Pentecost. Wow, wouldn't it be wonderful if God would pour out a fresh anointing upon His church? What if He would bring revival, and it would be like in New Testament days? So, I decided I would fast for fifty days. I realized that the fifty-day mark would be a Friday. But I wanted to fast until I had preached the Sunday morning services. So I continued for fifty-two days.

After I had preached those Sunday services, I went home, and that evening I opened my Bible to this passage in Haggai. God said, "This promise, this is for you." At 3 a.m., God told me to get up and read the word. I got up; I read Haggai chapter 2. Again, He said to me, "This promise is for you." I didn't understand it, so I began asking God to reveal His will to me as I studied it.

I'm going to share something that you may have never considered. I sometimes try to look at the numbers found in Scripture to see if they have any connection or significance to numerical details in my life. This is part of a Bible study technique called biblical numerology, where we carefully consider the numbers in a verse to see if there is a symbolic meaning behind them. So, as I was fasting for fifty-two days, I wondered if there was any significance to the number fifty-two in the Bible. I found the number fifty-two in the book of

Nehemiah. When Nehemiah got word from home about the condition of Jerusalem, that the walls were broken down, the gates had been burned, and his brothers were in trouble and disgrace, the Bible says that Nehemiah sat down and wept before God. He fasted to ask God to do something for his home city of Jerusalem. Nehemiah got permission from his king to go back to Jerusalem to rebuild the wall. It took him exactly fifty-two days to rebuild the wall (Nehemiah 6:15).

I got to thinking, *What if during my fifty-two-day fast something was happening in the spiritual realm?* I wondered if God was doing something in the supernatural that I wasn't aware of—that maybe God was going to take people who were really in trouble and give them a sense of hope. Maybe God was going to take people whose lives were in rubble and ruin and provide them with a safe place to heal. Could it be that God was going to build some spiritual walls in and around our city?

As I mentioned earlier, in 2006, I received a promise from the book of Haggai. As I was reading about Nehemiah, I began to see a connection back to the passage in Haggai. Nehemiah finished building the wall on the 25th day of the month. The passage in Haggai 2 says, "On the 24th day, from this day forward . . ." I realized that the 25th day was the next day after the 24th. It would be the first day of the blessing "from this day forward." I began to think about the whole concept of how God was orchestrating and bringing it together. Honestly, I thought the promise was for our church. I thought it was going to happen in 2006 or 2007. I had no idea that it would be 2016—ten years later—when God would begin to reveal the fulfillment of the promise He had given me on that day.

Stepping Out in Faith

I was the senior pastor at Brookville Road Community Church for thirty-three years—from 1983 to 2016. In 2015, after watching the video on the Dream Center's website and believing God was calling me to start something new, I began working with the board of elders and church staff on my succession plan. One night I was turning off the lights at the church when I felt sad to be leaving the church I loved and had given my life for. Some congregation members who had been at the church for decades—including my wife, children, and grandchildren—had to grieve this change for our church. I tried to reassure them that the church still had a wonderful staff leading it, and God was doing a new thing that would impact many in our city. In February 2016, I preached my last sermon at my church as the senior pastor and passed the baton on to the next lead pastor.

Then my son David and I stepped out in faith to create Hope Center Indy—a center that would impart hope and healing to every heart. We did not know how God was going to provide the money needed to pay staff salaries, the money to buy a building, or the money to fund the operating costs of the ministry. David was twenty-five years old at the time, but he had just graduated from Barclay College with a degree in Christian Ministries and from another local discipleship program called Revive School of Transformation. He had a radical faith in what God could do. I was so grateful God had prompted him to help me. I knew I needed him as a partner because of his earnest faith, enthusiasm, energy, and computer skills. (I have zero computer skills, so David became my secretary for a while...which he did not love, but he was willing to help as needed!)

David and I began to do research. How were we going to put this Hope Center together? I went to Los Angeles to the Dream Center and attended a conference where the keynote speaker was Pastor Tommy Barnett. After he spoke, I went up to introduce myself and explained that I was stepping out in faith to start the Hope Center. Tommy then prayed over me that God would use me to start a ministry like the Dream Center in our city.

We also visited the St. Louis Dream Center and the Evansville Dream Center. As we asked questions of those in leadership on these visits, we heard two recurring themes in their responses: (1) If you want to help someone, you have to get them out of their old environment. (2) If you want to help someone, you need to be able to do an aftercare program that is longer than thirty days. We learned that there certainly is a need for short-term emergency care shelters, short-term detox facilities, and short-term assessment programs. Still, there are not enough long-term restorative care facilities for these short-term facilities to refer people to. We began to see that thirty days was a good start, but if we really wanted to bring some healing into people's lives and fill a nationwide need that the country has for long-term restorative care, we would need to develop a program that would be much longer than thirty days. And this program would need to take a holistic approach.

Dave and I knew that we wanted to help people. We wanted to give people the support they needed to make a life change. So, we decided we would create an aftercare program that would be fifteen months long.

Then we had to decide who we were going to help. We learned there were more residential ministries in Indiana for men than women. So, we decided we would focus on helping women. In our research and to our knowledge at the time, there was no aftercare program in Indiana specifically for adult women exiting sex trafficking. Seeing this was an important need, we began to pray and ask God if He would open the door for us to meet this need.

David and I began to research sex trafficking. We read almost anything we could get our hands on to help inform us. I would like to pause here and share a few important facts about sex trafficking. Sex trafficking has become a more popular topic in recent years, and I am thankful that people are beginning to bring awareness to it and stand up against it. Here are a few things for you to consider:

- The International Labor Organization and Walk Free Foundation, in partnership with IOM, estimate that there are 4.8 million people trapped in forced sexual exploitation globally.[iii] While sex trafficking is a global problem, many people think that sex trafficking only happens overseas. But up to 300,000 people are caught in sex trafficking in America alone. Polaris Project publishes a map of the United States that shows the locations where human trafficking is happening. When we looked at the map and saw so much of our state of Indiana and our neighboring states covered in red, indicating a high volume of trafficking activity[iv], it made us realize that we couldn't just stand by and do nothing.

- The average age for the first time someone is trafficked in the U.S. is seventeen.[v] If we think about a seventeen-year-old that we know and care about, then we can begin to realize how tragic and evil it would be for that young person to be trapped and exploited at the young age when most people are starting to make dreams and plans for their lives. Since age seventeen is the average age, we recognize that many people are trafficked at even younger ages—young teens, preteens, and children.

- Traffickers prey on vulnerable people, which includes children, teens, and adults who have a history of sexual abuse, have a substance abuse issue or have a caregiver or family member who has a substance abuse issue, have a history of domestic violence, live in unstable living conditions, are runaways or are involved in the juvenile justice or foster care system, are facing poverty or economic need, or are undocumented immigrants.[vi]

As we considered the problem of sex trafficking, we knew that we wanted to help somehow. We began looking at facilities we could build out. We looked at vacant buildings in our area—an L.S. Ayres building, a Sears building, a K-mart building. Then, at the very same time that I stepped out from being the senior pastor at Brookville Road Community Church, a small college campus came on the market just a half mile down the road from our church.

Dave and I went to see this small college. We walked through the campus and could see that this place was exactly what we needed to be able to house residential ministries and outreach ministries. After the tour, we stopped looking at other buildings and started praying. We said, "God, this is it. We don't know how You're going to do this, but this is definitely where You want us to be." We began asking God to provide this campus for the ministry.

The only problem was that we were far from having the money to meet the purchase price. When I say to you that we were millions apart, we really were. I didn't know how God was going to work all that out, but we were constantly praying. We began inviting some friends from local churches to meet and pray with us every Wednesday evening to ask God to do something to help us to get this facility.

One day in July, we were sitting in our office, and we realized that the listing price from the owners was 5.45 million. For some reason, David said to me, "Dad, offer them 2 million dollars. We don't have 2 million dollars, but we can go ahead and offer it."

We wanted to see how they would respond to that offer. We had a realtor write the offer up and send it to them. A few weeks passed, and we didn't hear anything back from them. Finally, I called their attorney. "We sent an offer and haven't heard anything back."

He said, "Your offer was so low, we didn't even consider it."

I said, "Thank you for your time," and hung up.

Then Dave said, "Hey, Dad, offer them 3 million."

I thought, *We don't have 2 million or 3 million, so we might as well try.*

This time the owners countered back at 3.75 million. Not having the money, we knew it was time to pray even harder. We continued meeting with our prayer group on Wednesday evenings and continued seeking God on how He wanted to lead us.

Breaking through a Financial Wall

I became friends with Pastor Mark Wright and his wife Kathy when they were at the same Bible college with me in Kansas. We remained friends after college, and one day while I was praying in my prayer closet in 1991, I felt prompted to ask Mark and Kathy if they would be interested in planting our first church plant. They said yes and planted Brandywine Community Church, which is located about twenty miles from our church.

Mark and I have frequently worked together in missions and ministry. At the beginning of 2016, I began to tell Mark what God had put on my heart about starting the Hope Center and how David and I had toured a small college campus we believed would be the perfect place for us.

On the 25th day of September 2016, Pastor Mark was preaching a sermon at his church about their church's vision and goals for the next five years. My wife and I decided to go there that Sunday. I knew Mark had asked me for a picture of the college campus David and I had toured, but I didn't realize that God was leading him to talk about the Hope Center that morning. He began to speak about outreach and how their church was going to reach their community. When he was casting the vision, he took the picture of the college campus and put it on the large screen for the whole church to see. He said, "You see this—this is going to be the new Hope Center Indy. We're going to help these people get this building, and we're going to believe God will help this ministry become one of the largest aftercare programs in America for women survivors of sex trafficking."

Now, that was prophetic. That was the first time I had heard those words said out loud: "This is going to become one the largest aftercare programs for women survivors of sex trafficking in America." But because of the size of our campus, this was a realistic goal. There are only 1,300 beds in the nation for the 300,000 survivors of sex trafficking. [vii]

Mark was preaching that morning, on the 25th day of September. (I can remember it pretty easily because it was my birthday.) This relates back to the promise that God gave me in 2006 from Haggai 2:18–19: "From this day forward, I'm going to bless you." On that day, Mark pointed to the picture of the campus on the screen, and he said, "This is going to be Hope Center Indy. We're going to help them get this facility, and God's going to do this. Let's stop right now and all of us are going to pray." He stopped right in the middle of his message: "God, please, we need a breakthrough. We need you to do something. Help us, please, God.'" He prayed that God would break through our financial wall, not just during the first service, but in both services.

The next day, Monday, I got a call from the campus's attorney. The attorney asked me, "Are you guys interested in leasing the facility?"

"Yes," I replied. "I didn't realize that was an option."

He said, "Put some kind of lease agreement together and send it to me."

I didn't want to offend them—I think I had already offended them with my last few offers to buy the campus. But I put an offer together for a lease agreement to present to their board and sent it to them on Wednesday.

On Friday, I was actually farming because our crops were ready to be harvested. (As I mentioned in a previous chapter, my brother and I farm together.) But I noticed that the attorney's number came up on my phone. So, I stopped and turned the tractor off. I answered the phone, and the attorney said, "We want you to know that the board approved leasing you the facility."

Once I got off the phone with the attorney, I got out of the tractor. I went to the edge of the field, stood with my hands in the air, and said, "Lord, thank you—I think. I'm not quite sure!"

I had just taken over a 210,000-square-foot facility, a 25-acre campus, and a monthly lease payment of $10,500. I was thinking, *I'm not sure whether this is a good thing or not. I think this is a good thing . . . I think.*

Looking back, I realize that when Pastor Mark prayed with his church on September 25, God brought forth the fulfillment of His promise given to me ten years earlier in 2006: "From the ninth month the 24th day, from this day forward I will bless you."

The Promise Starts to Come Alive with the New Campus!

We ended up taking over the facility in November 2016. David and I drove up to the new Hope Center campus together that first day in November. It was hard to believe that God was entrusting us with this facility, but we knew this was not about us. This was about God doing something for the women who would eventually come live on campus as residents and find hope in Christ. Yet, on that first day, it was just Dave and me and a few meager office supplies. The verse of Zechariah 4:10 was certainly for us: "Do not despise these small beginnings." The following year, Dave wrote about our first day driving up to our campus and posted it to our Hope Center blog. He titled his blog post "Day 1. Overwhelmed & Excited."

"My name is David Nolen. I am the Co-founder/Associate Director at Hope Center Indy, and

I want to share with you my experience of the first day on campus.

I've always admired my dad's faith when it comes to following God's path for his life. The core belief that God longs and wants to use His people to do impossible things has propelled him to where he is today. He constantly dreams BIG with a prayer life that matches his big dreams pound for pound. I've sat in several hours of long prayer sessions with my dad. Over the years, I've heard him pouring out his heart to the Lord, interceding for those who are lost, praying for those who are brokenhearted, crying out for a revival, and most importantly just listening & believing God is going to do great and mighty things. Witnessing this faith as his son over the years has been a priceless blessing. It was my joy to carry this experience into day one at the Hope Center Indy campus.

After signing the lease agreement, we pulled up to the 25-acre campus together, not many words being said between us. We were both still in shock. As we pulled up, I remember feeling like Simba from the Lion King when Mufasa said to his son, "Look, Simba, everything the light touches is our kingdom." This 25-acre, 210,000-square-foot campus just seemed enormous and never-ending! How could anyone manage this entire place?!! All these what-ifs and how-am-I-going-tos flooded my mind instantly. I must have looked like a man afraid of his own shadow, staring at this building.

If you have ever been overwhelmed by the size of the dream God has for you, then you probably know the look I had in my eyes. It's the look of "I know I'm not supposed to feel fearful, but I can't help it, God." It's almost like God has a Ph.D. in surprising us with dreams He knows will make us feel overwhelmed. Just take Habakkuk 1:5, for example. It says, "Look at the nations and watch, and be utterly amazed. For I am going to do something in your days that you would not believe, even if you were told." This verse is special to me for many reasons. In 2013 God spoke this verse to me in a season when I had no idea what to do with my life. Then three years go by, and I'm staring at this 25-acre campus in utter amazement while God is doing something in my days I certainly wouldn't have believed, even if I had been told.

Looking over at my dad, I could see him grinning like he was excited for the challenge. Like he was complimenting God on the interesting journey up to this point, realizing this was going to be fun to watch God come through in miraculous ways. My overwhelmed feeling went away as I began to feel excited too. Excited to experience the highs and lows of this next chapter. Excited to begin something new. Excited that we couldn't

make this happen without heavy involvement from God.
My dad often quotes Angus Buchan saying, "When men
work, men work. But when men pray, God works!"

Moving Into Our New Campus

Driving up that first day to the campus and getting out of
the car with my son David was one of the happiest days of
my life. To be able to go on this faith journey with him was
everything a father could hope for! As we stood at the front
door, I wondered what Dave was thinking and feeling. How
was his faith doing? This adventure with Jesus would be the
greatest test of my faith, his faith, and both of our faiths
together! I stood there, knowing that if God didn't do this, it
wouldn't get done!

As we sat alone in the office with just our old desk, my
iPad, and his laptop, we prayed and wondered who God
would send to partner with us in ministry. God was at work,
and people started gaining interest in the vision for the Hope
Center.

One day, not long after David and I had moved in, a
gentleman asked if we could use some office furniture.

I said, "Yes, we could."

So, he picked me up and took me to a pharmaceutical
company. He told me that they were moving campuses. He
said to go in and pick out anything we wanted. I marked
thirty-five offices with furniture, which were each originally

purchased for $8,400. He told me to come back the next day, so I did and marked twenty more offices. Then a company representative finally told me to start sending semitrailers, and he would give it all to me.

They sent us nine semitrailers full of office furniture—desks, chairs, and conference tables. They even gave us their commercial kitchen, which we were able to then give away to an inner-city school that needed it. We were able to stage thirty offices, which was every office we had at the Hope Center. Dave and I looked at each other and realized that God had a bigger plan than we did because He had provided desks and chairs for every office. This was an indicator to us that He was going to send people to come work with us in those offices.

We were also able to give to nonprofits and churches. We began to be a blessing to other people. All of a sudden, we got to say, "From this day forward, God's going to bless the Hope Center."

David and I then carried our old, broken-down desk outside, busted it up with a sledgehammer, and threw it in the dumpster. We said, "Thank you, Jesus, for this wonderful blessing!" This gift from the pharmaceutical company was likely valued at around $500,000. Even today, when people see our office furniture, we can remind them of this first miraculous provision for the Hope Center Indy campus.

About five months after we had moved into our new campus, Pastor Mark asked me to come back to preach at Brandywine Community Church. He said their church would take up an offering for the Hope Center. The following Sunday, which was Easter Sunday, Brandywine took up an offering for us—it amounted to over $25,000. I remember that day. As they passed the buckets to take up the offering, Tonia and I just wept. For all of our lives, we have given by planting churches and giving away. Now we were on the receiving end of this incredible blessing. Mark was saying, "We're going to make these people winners. We're going to move the kingdom of God forward." And they did!

Another Confirmation

About two years after that, a group from the Hope Center, including new residents, went to hear Pastor Tommy Barnett preach at a church about thirty miles from our campus. I was able to go backstage to introduce myself and talk to him about the Hope Center and how his vision for the Dream Center in L.A. had inspired me to start our ministry. Then our group wanted to sit in the front row of the audience while he spoke. During his message, Pastor Barnett surprised the crowd by jumping off the stage. He walked over to me and said, "You can do more. Hubert, you can do more, so go on and do it!"

I was surprised by his challenge to me—I felt like I had just given my all to get the ministry to this point! But then I loved his heart of faith and the message of that challenge: Go on! What promise are you still waiting for God to fulfill? Go on! Keep believing the promises. You can do more!

Promises to Read:

Psalm 16:3: "I say of the holy people who are in the land, 'They are the noble ones in whom is all my delight.'"

Proverbs 3:5–6: "Trust in the LORD with all your heart and lean not on your own understanding; in all your ways submit to him, and he will make your paths straight."

Jeremiah 42:3: "Pray that the LORD your God will tell us where we should go and what we should do."

James 1:5: "If any of you lacks wisdom, you should ask God, who gives generously to all without finding fault, and it will be given to you."

Prayer to Pray:

Lord, do You want me to step out and follow You into a new ministry? I ask You to grant me Your wisdom and guidance. Give me a promise from Your word that I can stand upon and trust in. Do great things through my life. In Jesus' name, Amen.

Aerial View of Hope Center Indy campus

6

An Army Showed Up!

Taking over the 210,000 square feet of building space at the Hope Center was intimidating. One of the first things Dave and I did was paint and get our offices ready. We put two coats of paint on the walls, painted the trim, and cleaned our carpet. (Did I mention that our carpet is red? Dave was not a fan of the red carpet. I think it kept him awake at night thinking of how it was hard to match furniture, paint, etc.)

It took us all week to get our offices ready for the furniture. At the end of that week, we were tired, and I was so grateful to be finished.

Then it dawned on me that we had twenty-eight more offices to do just like ours! At this rate, if Dave and I had done all the offices ourselves, it would have taken us four months. This wasn't even counting the eighty residential bedrooms, five classrooms, several workspaces, hallways for all three floors, etc. I prayed, *Lord, we need help! Please send an army to help us!*

Better Together

While I pastored, I dreamed of a church where every member was involved in helping accomplish the Great Commission, found in Matthew 28:19, to: "Go and make disciples of all nations." When I was at Brookville Road Community Church, I didn't want just a small percentage of the people in our church having all the fun, receiving all the blessings, and gaining all the rewards. I wanted everyone who attended our church to get in on God's wonderful blessing of being a co-laborer with Him. I wanted everyone to experience the life change that comes from serving, to know the joy of doing something for a greater cause, and to change the eternal destiny of people we may or may not ever meet.

I fell in love with Jesus when I gave my life to Him at the age of twenty. I fell in love with His church somewhere along my pastoral journey as I watched His followers live out their love for Him. It has been said that the local church is the hope of the world when she is working correctly. I have seen her shine in her beauty, radiate hope, and be the instrument of redemption for humanity. But I have also seen her at her worst when the wheels fall off, and we try to lead the church with our own understanding instead of the wisdom of God, when we are self-led instead of Spirit-led. But when we get it right, the bride of Christ is beautiful in all her splendor.

Many years ago, I learned about the Pareto principle, which is the 80/20 rule of cause and effect. Eighty percent of outcomes (outputs) come from twenty percent of causes (inputs). I didn't want the 80/20 rule—where 80% of the work is done by 20% of the people—to be true of my church.

I didn't want 20% of the church members doing 80% of our mission. I realize we are all different. We have different gifts, passions, and personalities. One person may be low-energy while another might have a type A personality, driven to succeed and to accomplish. Yet no matter the talent, gift, or personality type, we each need to take our one and only life and use it to make a difference. While it doesn't always come out to be an exact 80/20 ratio, we can see this imbalance in business: Twenty percent of salespeople make eighty percent of the total sales. Twenty percent of customers generate eighty percent of the revenue. Twenty percent of the workforce is accomplishing eighty percent of all the work. During twenty percent of your workday, you accomplish eighty percent of your work.

We all want to do something that matters—something that will go on after we are gone. We all want to leave our mark and leave a legacy. So, let's do it together.

Before I go on to share about how God sent so many wonderful people to work together at the Hope Center, I want to rewind to tell a story from 2005 that taught me so much about this principle of how God's people can accomplish great things when we work together. In 2005, at Brookville Road Community Church, we did a series called "40 Days of Community" by Saddleback Church and Pastor Rick Warren. The main emphasis was to impact our community for Jesus and realize we are better together and can accomplish so much more when we join hands.

During the series, I drove onto the campus and saw a group of retired men from our church working and painting the trim around the church windows. As I got out of the car, I walked over to thank these men for their service. They all stopped their tasks for a few minutes to chat with me. They smiled and said, "Pastor, we have a paint brush that will fit your hand if you want to join us."

I know these men really enjoyed working and serving together. Our conversation may have been the highlight of their service day. I know it was a highlight for me. As I thanked them for serving and donating their time, a gentleman reached out his hand to shake mine and said, "Pastor, we are better together."

I said, "Yes, we are, and you guys make me look better than I really am." As I walked into my office, I thought, *Wow, this group of men gets it.* We are better together and can accomplish more as the body of Christ when all its members are serving.

Impacting the Community

During the "40 Days of Community" sermon series in 2005, I asked a lady named Missy in our church to do some research for me. I wanted to know how much it would cost to provide food for all the families in need in our county for forty days. She reached out to the local food pantry, and they came up with a total of $17,000. On Sunday morning, I challenged our church to raise the $17,000 needed, and we did! We wanted to get the whole church involved, so Missy went to work on a purchase plan. Working with a local food distributor, we were able to purchase the food that was needed. I can't remember how many pallets of food were delivered, but it was a lot. They placed them in the large cafe area of our church where everyone enters. Every item needed to be marked with an expiration date, so we asked for volunteers to help.

Looking at all those pallets and all the items on each pallet, I thought, *This could take forever. What have we gotten ourselves into?* I had a meeting that evening, so I was planning to do my meeting, then go out to the cafe and help tackle what seemed to me an impossible task. Volunteers showed up and began to work. When my meeting was over, I finally journeyed out to help in the cafe. To my surprise, the lights were off, everyone was gone, and the goal had already been accomplished. I could hardly believe my eyes! How had they done this? A mighty army of volunteers descended on the pallets and made short work of what would have taken a few people days or even a week.

I just stood there smiling and thinking, *Wow, what we can do together!*

We delivered the food to the local food pantry, and it didn't last just forty days—it lasted for ninety days! Missy was so inspired that she joined the board of the local food pantry. She started an annual fundraiser called Harvest for the Hungry. Each year our church hosted a silent auction with a catered meal and a guest speaker. In the first year, Missy and the Harvest for the Hungry's volunteer team raised $20,000 to keep the pantry stocked with food. Then Missy grew the number of supporters for the Harvest for the Hungry and maxed out our seating capacity at 500, and she did this for ten years. As a church, together with our community and local businesses, we all came together for a common cause: to stop hunger in our community. Over those ten years, Missy and her amazing team of volunteers raised over $500,000 to impact lives. It never ceases to amaze me what can be done when we enlist as volunteers in God's mighty army. We needed this kind of volunteerism at the Hope Center if we were going to succeed in this major undertaking. We needed many people with hearts like Missy.

Daunting Task for Two

Dave and I wanted the Hope Center to be God's ministry funded by Him and founded on His biblical principles. We wanted His church to help in the responsibility to combat human trafficking. If churches worldwide won't pick up this responsibility, then who will? If not His servants, then who will be willing to bring light into this darkness? Dave and I started to pray for 100 churches to come on board to help us at the Hope Center. We counted them as partners if they sent volunteers to do work projects, gave us a one-time gift during the year, or supported us monthly through their mission or outreach budget.

Dave and I went anywhere and everywhere to get the word out about the ministry of the Hope Center. I don't even know how many churches we spoke at over the first couple of years. We attended lunch appointments for business associations, rotary clubs, toastmasters, lions clubs, ladies' groups, etc. We cast the vision and told people, "We need you to come and help us."

We have three separate buildings on our campus. As we worked on various parts of the buildings, I kept praying about putting the Prayer Center together. The 5,000-square-foot space we were going to use for the Prayer Center had originally been a beautiful facility with red carpet and beautiful woodwork. But we had a problem—the roof had leaked, and the water damage had ruined it all. A volunteer group from a local church called Park Chapel Christian Church came in one Saturday for a workday, and they gutted the whole building and cleaned it up. The building was left with just a concrete floor and a block ceiling.

After we got that space all gutted and ready to go, I made a list in my mind of what we still needed to do: stain the concrete floor, put a drop ceiling in, build a little platform for the worship teams, install a furnace and air conditioning unit, hang drywall, and paint the walls. I figured I could do this for $20,000. I know, I'm an eternal optimist who thinks he can get something done cheaper than he can actually get it done for.

One day I was talking to the Lord about what we needed to do in the Prayer Center. I said, "Lord, we need about $20,000, so what are You going to do about this? This is Your ministry."

This doesn't happen to me very often, but in that moment, I felt the Lord bring a lady's name to my mind, and I heard Him say to me, "Ask her."

I knew this lady had been on a tour, and I knew she had a heart for who we were. But I certainly didn't feel like I knew her well enough to ask her for $20,000.

I went to my office, and I found her contact information. I sat down and put a text message together. "I'm trying to raise $20,000 for the Prayer Center, and your name was the first name that came to my mind. I have other people I can ask to help with this, but I wanted to see if you and your husband might consider praying about helping me with the Prayer Center." I sat there for a long time before sending the text message. I thought, *This is crazy. Do you even send something like this?? I don't even know these people that well.* Finally, I made my finger hit send.

Five minutes later, this lady texted me back: "We would be honored to give you $20,000 for your Prayer Center."

As I was sitting in my chair, I dropped my phone on the carpet. *Are you serious? Wow!*

God speaks all the time. Sometimes we might think, *That was just my voice. I think I came up with that thought . . . surely that wasn't God saying something to me.* But the only way we can know for sure whether it was God or not is by obeying the prompting. And when we obey the prompting, we can see the result. If we never obey the prompting, we will never know if it was God or not. Usually, a prompting won't feel like He spoke so clearly that you will automatically know it was Him.

In this instance, I just felt like it had to be the Lord speaking, and I followed through.

There were many more incredible moments in the development of the Prayer Center: A man came to the Hope Center who worked for a drywall company. He was helping figure out how much material we would need to drywall the building. When he got it all figured out, he said, "Pastor, I'm so busy, I can't do this myself. But I tell you what I will do. I will give you all the drywall materials you need, and I'll have my crew deliver it out here to you tomorrow."

I thought, "Okay, sounds pretty good. That's better than what I had."

Standing beside me that day was another gentleman. When he heard the other guy say, "I will give you all the drywall you need," he said to me, "If he's going to give you the drywall, I will pay to have it hung and finished." The first gentleman had his crew deliver all that drywall. They stacked it for us on the inside of the building. And that second gentleman paid for another crew to come hang and finish the drywall.

I was sitting in my office one day shortly after that, and my phone rang. A guy said to me, "What are you doing?"

I told him that I was getting ready to go to a paint store to buy paint for the Prayer Center. He said, "If you're going to pick it up, I will pay for it." His phone call came at just the right time. I drove to the paint store, feeling thankful again for how God was providing for every detail.

We saw those types of things continue to happen as we got the Prayer Center up and going. Several people came together to make it happen. For instance, all the electric supplies, lights, and hours of electrical work were donated. All the carpet, chairs, and sound equipment we needed were given to us with a generous heart.

The Prayer Center renovation actually came in under budget because of peoples' generous and miraculous contributions.

We have an enclosed walkway with a glass roof and glass windows as walls that connects our boutique to our Prayer Center. We call it "The Prayer Tunnel" because it leads to the Prayer Center, and we have small banners with Scripture passages on prayer that people can read as they walk through. (You can see our "Prayer Tunnel" in the photos included in this book.) It is a beautiful sight to stand at the entrance of the glass tunnel and look through it, especially when it is all lit up for our Christmas season. I thought, *Wouldn't it be a great idea to honor our partners with a plaque with the name of their church on it?* I met Jen, a wonderful Christian lady who does woodworking as a labor of love back to our Lord. I asked her if she would be willing to create small, beautiful wooden plaques with the churches' names on the front to place on the window ledges of the Prayer Tunnel. She eagerly said yes, and over the last couple of years, she has dropped off boxes of new plaques to display.

I give tours of our campus on Saturdays, and we start in our boutique and then walk through "The Prayer Tunnel" to the Prayer Center. As we walk the tunnel, our visitors look for their church's plaque in the windows. When they find it, they often stop and take a picture with their church plaque. They are so proud their church has partnered with us to fight human trafficking. If they don't see their church's name, I tell them, "I need you to go back and share with your church about this kingdom-minded ministry that is bringing churches together to change lives and our city."

As I mentioned earlier, as we moved on campus in 2016, Dave and I first started praying for 100 churches to come on board and help us. Today we have 158. So now we are praying for two hundred. Each week we pray for the churches which line our tunnel, asking our Heavenly Father to bless them for blessing us.

A Different Kind of Army

I had no idea what kind of buy-in we would have from our local business community. I now realize that most businesses have a core value of giving back or serving their community. They want to team up with nonprofits that are making a difference, so they have come to the Hope Center to volunteer. Groups of 10, 20, 50, 100, or even 200 have come to our campus to do service projects (such as landscaping, painting, construction projects, deep cleaning, etc.) to help us keep moving forward. They have opened their hearts and wallets to donate hundreds and thousands of dollars over the last five years. The businesses along with church groups have donated around 400,000 volunteer hours. If each volunteer was paid $10 an hour to volunteer, and if we have had 400,000 hours served, it would amount to about a 4-million-dollar gift to God's ministry. These volunteers have saved us millions of dollars and have given us the opportunity to get to know some great people. One of my greatest joys of serving at the center is getting to meet so many of God's wonderful people and to see them in action: putting on their work clothes and gloves and getting invested in this work.

One day I was at a restaurant, sharing with an older gentleman about the Hope Center. I told him, "Every single day is a God day. A day of answers to prayer, miracles, wonders, a new day with partnerships, networking, joining together with others for a greater cause. Every day God is doing something—He's moving and He's blessing. Every day is a God day."

We talked for a couple of hours, and when we got up from our table to leave, I saw a young man sitting at his table across the room. I knew him from Brandywine Community

Church and had been close with his family. He walked over to me and shook my hand. He said, "Pastor, the Lord's been dealing with me to mow the Hope Center campus."

I said, "Wait a minute. Do you know that it's twenty-five acres?"

He said, "Like I said, the Lord's been dealing with me to mow the campus. Just let me take care of it."

I turned to walk with the older gentleman, and I told him, "Like I said, every day is a God day at the Hope Center. God is meeting our needs left and right. Every day becomes a day of blessing."

From 2017-2020, that young man mowed all 25 acres of the Hope Center campus. He was yet another incredible partner who used the resources and abilities God gave him to serve at the Hope Center.

Washer and Dryer

Bonnie was an older lady in her seventies who had cancer. She hosted a prayer group in her home every Sunday at 5:00 p.m.

I came home on a Sunday afternoon, and Bonnie called me and said, "Pastor, my prayer group is getting ready to meet and pray. We wanted to know what we could pray for for the Hope Center."

I thought, *What do I tell this lady about what to pray for?* We had a long list of needs, and it was hard to choose just one thing and say, "Pray about this." I thought about it and finally decided on something to share with her.

I told her, "We have volunteers who are helping us do laundry. They wash the bedding, tablecloths, and towels to prepare for when residents move in, and they have told me that we could use some commercial washers and dryers. All the washers and dryers the Center has are from its previous occupants. They are for residential use, and they are all old and really worn out. So, if we could get a couple sets of commercial washers and dryers, that would be a big blessing for us."

She said, "Thank you," and then prayed about that with her group that evening. That group prayed about it and shared that need with some friends. The word must have gotten around because a couple weeks later, the executive pastor from The Creek Church called me and said, "We would like to provide you with two sets of commercial washers and dryers."

I told them that would be great! They came with a group of people, and I gave them a tour of the building. Then they presented me with a check for $5,000.

A few weeks later, I was giving another tour to another group of people. I told them this story of how Bonnie and her prayer group had prayed specifically for us to receive new sets of commercial washers and dryers and how the pastor at The Creek Church then gave us a check for $5,000 to cover the cost of them.

In this group on this tour, there was a lady who said, "Pastor, please let me help you. That's what I do—I sell appliances. There are appliances out there that will get makeup and stains out of pillowcases and sheets, and if you get those, you will be really happy with how they work. I'll come in. I'll present the options to you, and you can decide which washers and dryers you would like to purchase."

A few weeks later, she made an appointment with me. She came to my office, sat down at my desk, and said, "Pastor, this is exactly what you need. It's top of the line. It will do everything you need it to do, and our company will give it to you at our cost—we won't make anything from this sale. The cost is $3,700."

I thought, *This is a pretty good deal. We've already received the check for $5,000, so we'll have some of that money left over to use on other needs.*

At the end of her presentation, she said asked, "Could I share with you why I want to serve here at the Hope Center?"

I smiled and said, "Of course."

She paused for a moment, then tears came to the surface of her eyes. She said, "About a year ago, my daughter was sexually assaulted. And it devastated our lives." She told me the story of how they were trying to put their lives back together and how they were trying to heal from all they had endured. My heart broke for her family.

After she finished her story, we discussed how the Hope Center can be a tangible reminder that God gives hope in even life's hardest moments. Before she got up to leave, she looked up at me and said, "Pastor, if I were to pay for the washers and dryers, do you think you could use the money from the church for something else?"

I was reminded once again that God wanted to impart hope and healing to all of us—not just the residents. This lady went on to buy the washers and dryers for us herself, and I pray that this sacrificial gift will help bring hope and healing to her heart and her family.

After she left my office, I realized that God had just provided a double portion. Sometimes God shows us that He will meet our needs—and not only that, but He will meet them a couple times over.

At the end of our tours, people often say to me, "Thank you. This is so encouraging to see and hear. We had no idea that people still cared enough to sacrifice their time and money. Our hearts are challenged to do something ourselves."

One of the most inspiring things about the Hope Center is how this incredible army from central Indiana and beyond showed up to make a difference for women overcoming human trafficking. I continue to be humbled by the church groups, business groups, volunteers, and donors who have joined us to make the Hope Center ministry possible. I love that so many people have been blessed by being part of something bigger than themselves. It causes me to rejoice and praise God for His wonderful people. When we join hands for a common cause, we can achieve things none of us can achieve on our own. Little did I realize when I started the Hope Center that I would see a ministry where the volunteerism was what I had hoped for. I had dreamed that not just a small percentage, but that everyone could be part of an eternal blessing. Thank you, mighty army, for showing up to help create the Hope Center!

Promises to Read:

Ecclesiastes 4:9: "Two are better than one, because they have a good return for their labor."

Matthew 28:19-20: "Therefore go and make disciples of nations, baptizing them in the name of the Father and of the Son and of the Holy Spirit, and teaching them to obey everything I have commanded you. And surely I am with you always, to the very end of the age."

Mark 10:45: "For even the Son of Man did not come to be served, but to serve, and to give his life as a ransom for many."

Prayer to Pray:

Heavenly Father, I ask for discernment. Please show me where you would have me volunteer. I want to give my life for something greater than myself. I want to do something eternal and have a lasting impact. Make me a servant like Jesus. In Jesus' name, Amen.

Bedroom that was adopted by a volunteer group to prepare it for future residents

*Bedroom that was adopted by a volunteer
group to prepare it for future residents*

Volunteer Group at HCI

Prayer Tunnel lights at night.

Prayer Tunnel leading to Prayer Center

7

Wait 'Til Monday and See What God Will Do

During the Spring of 2017, Dave and I continued to cast the vision of Hope Center Indy becoming a residential program for women survivors of sex trafficking. People began stepping up as financial partners to help us take steps toward this vision. These financial gifts enabled us to hire a program director and a few program staff members. As we prepared the building, we also were preparing our program team with trainings on human trafficking, trauma, substance abuse recovery, and residential care.

We realized that clothing would be one of the immediate needs for the ladies who would come into our residential program. Our new program staff members knew from their research and experience that many of the women who would become Hope Center residents would be fleeing their traffickers and would not have the opportunity to pack their things. They knew other women would be coming straight from jail or a drug rehabilitation center. Each woman's story would be different, but whatever the situation, we wanted to be prepared to have clothes available for the women who came.

We wanted to do something better than having a closet full of thrift clothes for the women to rummage through. I am no expert on fashion (my wife buys all of my clothes!), so this aspect of ministry was *not* part of the skill set I learned from working my pig farm. Thankfully, I have four daughters, and they told me that nice outfits, good shoes, and fun accessories like jewelry and purses could help the women regain a feeling of self-worth and a desire to make a new start.

Two volunteers came to me to address this need for clothing for the residents. One was my daughter Rachel, and the other was her good friend and longtime member of our church, Sarah. One day Rachel and Sarah said to me, "What if we started a women's boutique here? It could provide clothing for the residents and be an ongoing fundraiser for the Center."

Now, the funny thing was I had never heard of a boutique, never been to a boutique, and could hardly pronounce the word *boutique*. Yet, these two ladies convinced me it was worth trying. They set out to create the Redefined Hope Boutique in the front entrance of our main building. What was wonderful to me was that they were doing it with their own money. There was no start-up budget for the Boutique (just like there was no start-up budget for the Hope Center!).

Everything had to begin with steps of faith. So, as women in their thirties with young families, Rachel and Sarah sacrificed their own money and eventually left their jobs to make this dream happen. They looked at this 25-acre campus and began to realize the massive amount of necessary upkeep and required expense to create and maintain this ministry. By faith, Rachel and Sarah's goal was to make the Boutique a giving engine to pay the Hope Center's monthly lease payment of $10,500. So, they started working toward this goal using their God-given gifts of design, fashion, and presentation. They gathered what they could find on our campus, such as antiques, tables, and other things they might be able to use for their setup. They built things using a hammer and a drill and began to create two rooms in which to house the Boutique.

Adopt a Room

As they worked on the Boutique, we were also getting the building ready for our future residents. One day on a tour, a lady asked me, "Can we adopt a room?"

"Yes," I said. "What a great idea!"

That's when we started a program called "Adopt a Room." We provided the paint and bed frames; otherwise, the individuals, businesses, small groups, and families would adopt bedrooms and provide all the bedding, decor, bathroom necessities, window treatments, etc., to make the rooms look beautiful. We had two goals in mind: We wanted a new resident to walk into her new bedroom and feel valued. We also wanted her to realize that people she may never meet cared about her because she is worth being cared for! The heart and love these volunteers put into these rooms was above and beyond any expectations we had. One of our residents would later tell me that she would joke with her family that even though she was only twenty years old, she lived in an eighty-two-room mansion! She could feel the love that had been poured into her bedroom, the living rooms, and meeting rooms.

After a room is finished, there may be a waiting period before a new resident arrives to occupy it. During that in-between time, we sometimes show our guests on tours the finished adopted room. When people see these rooms, they are in awe of how beautiful and detailed they are.

God Even Has Exit Lights

One day our maintenance director, Bob, informed me that we needed to replace some of our exit lights before our fire inspection. I said, "Sure, how much?"

I was thinking it would be a couple hundred dollars. But Bob said the exit lights would be $1,100. Wow! I guess when you have a 210,000-square-foot facility, you need a lot of exit lights. Reluctantly, I approved the expenditure, and over the next few weeks, the new exit lights were all installed.

One day a gentleman came through our building, and I mentioned that we had just replaced all the exit lights. As I listened to what he said next, a faith light turned on for me. He said, "Our company could have provided you with all the exit lights you needed." I looked at this man and realized there was a powerful lesson that I needed to learn about God: God even has exit lights! He has everything. We just need to pray about everything. It had never dawned on me that God would want to be actively involved in every minute detail of the Center. I was going to see God's mighty hand of provision like I had never seen in forty years of pastoral ministry. God would delight in providing in ways that only He could.

As Rachel, Sarah, and other volunteers painted and created the Boutique, they were getting closer to completion. On a Thursday, Sarah came into my office and showed me a sample of the flooring. It was a dark wood laminate. She said, "Pastor, this is the flooring we have picked out. It is $2,000 for the materials, not counting the labor. What should we do?"

What she was saying was that they didn't have this kind of money, so they needed help with the cost of the flooring. I am a slow learner, and too often I just want to take things into my own hands. But for some reason, when Sarah asked me about the flooring, I remembered the exit lights and how God could have provided those if I had only prayed about it. I said to Sarah, "I tell you what we are going to do: We are going to pray and say, 'God, You have until Monday to provide flooring because if You don't, we will have to buy it.'"

Sarah looked at me, and with like-minded faith, she said, "I'm good with that. Let's pray and see what God does."

We didn't spend hours praying about it. We just said a few simple prayers over the next day or so. Little did we know that God would hear and act on those simple prayers!

A God Moment with Flooring

The Saturday after my conversation with Sarah about the flooring, I was giving a tour at the Hope Center. At the Center we are trying to do something unique. In order to bring lots of people together to accomplish a big goal, we work to partner with the public in the cause of helping survivors of human trafficking. To do this, we give tours of our campus every Saturday. We try to raise awareness about how human trafficking occurs in the U.S. and also share about our fifteen-month program that helps lead residents to faith, healing, and purpose.

During this day's tour (two days after Sarah and I had talked about the flooring), I pointed to the area Rachel and Sarah were working on and said, "These two rooms over here will be the Redefined Hope Boutique. It will be an ongoing fundraiser every day for the Hope Center. As soon as we get the flooring down, we will be ready to go."

A man in the tour group spoke right up and said, "I will buy the flooring and install it if you'll let me."

Wanting to make sure I had heard him correctly, I asked, "Did you say you would buy the flooring and install it *if I let you*?"

He responded, "That's exactly what I said."

I smiled and said to him, "I will let you!"

Two days later, on Monday, he came in carrying the flooring and installed it in the area designated for the Boutique. I enjoy praying, but an even greater joy is when you get to be an answer to prayer. When this man came in that day, I don't think he had any idea that he was the answer to a prayer we had prayed. When I pray, I often say, "God, please do this, and please use me if You want to." I think many of us have found that it is a great joy when He wants to use us to meet a need!

126

This man, like most of our volunteers, was an average hard-working guy who had a family to provide for. Even with his tight schedule and budget, he wanted to be part of God's work, so he made this sacrifice of time and money. We know God blessed him for it. This man told me later that he had received a promotion and was now in a supervisory position for his career.

This provision was a surprise gift to us. God showed us that He could provide for our exact needs if we only prayed about them. This gift was worth far more than the $2,000 flooring cost because it boosted my faith and the faith of our other staff members.

After this smile from God, we created this motto at the Center: "Let's wait 'til Monday and see what God will do."

This is the first "God story" that we now share on our tours. It always brings smiles and laughter. For some, it lets them know that God is present, and God delights in answering our prayers. For those on a journey toward faith, it causes them to stop and consider that maybe God is real and God cares. If God answers prayers here, then maybe He'll answer prayers for them. We don't know just how many seeds of faith have been planted into the hearts of people based on this one story.

Wait Upon the Lord

I wish I could say in life's class of waiting that I have always gotten an A, but to be honest, at times, I have flunked. No one likes waiting around. The waiting room of life is where life seems to drag on, and we feel we are wasting our precious time. Yet in Psalm 27:4, King David says, "Wait on the Lord, be strong and take heart and wait on the Lord." I usually feel impatient when a project is creeping along, and it appears very little is being done. King David encourages us to take the spiritual discipline of waiting very seriously. Even though we learn throughout the Bible that waiting is a very profitable investment of our time, we too often fail to wait upon the Lord. Why is this so hard? For me, it feels like waiting is wasting, waiting is failing, or waiting is poor leadership. Waiting goes against the grain of leadership, like swimming upstream or walking into the strong wind. It feels like waiting for any amount of time is counterproductive. Leaders are movers and shakers. They are the people who move the dial and push the envelope. They get the job done.

As Americans, we want instant everything. Several years ago, I helped bring my friend Paul from another country to the U.S. to get his college education. On arriving in America, I thought he should experience some great American food. I should have given him my mom's apple pie or her German chocolate cake. Instead, I took him to White Castle, thinking he should taste their well-known sandwich and french fries.

In Indiana, White Castle serves small hamburgers with onions and pickles. You either love them, or you hate them.

Since we were in a hurry (of course—all Americans are), we went to the drive-through. I ordered, drove up to the window, paid, and they handed me our order. The drive-through attendant said, "Sorry for the wait."

It hadn't taken two or three minutes total from ordering to receiving. Paul laughed, "Sorry for the wait? Are you kidding? It was only a few minutes!"

As Americans, we are so used to getting something quickly that if it doesn't happen immediately, we expect people to say, "Sorry for the wait."

Today I went to the drive-through at our local bank to make a deposit. I put my deposit in the canister and pushed the button for it to fly inside to a waiting teller. She greeted me and told me she would be right back. After just a couple of minutes had passed, she came back to the window and said, "My computer crashed, and another lady is doing your deposit. We are so sorry for your wait."

Unlike the White Castle drive-through attendant and the bank teller, King David says he is *not* sorry for the wait. Twice in verse 14, he says, "Wait upon the Lord!" To wait upon the Lord and His timing keeps us from taking things into our own hands, doing things by our own effort instead of learning to be led by the Holy Spirit.

Praying and waiting upon the Lord is something I need to put into practice every day at the Hope Center. It is a large campus with many financial needs. The facility maintenance, the residents, and the staff all require attention. This "class" on waiting is a good life lesson in how God wants to work in and through our lives to show His favor. When celebrating what God had done at the Hope Center, my son David would say, "When we needed drywall work, God knew a guy. When we needed a plumber, God knew a guy. When we needed an electrician, God knew a guy. When we needed a lawn mower, God knew a guy." Whatever we need, God knows a guy or gal who can fill the need! Our Hope Center staff have learned that God will bring people's skills and resources together in His timing to accomplish His work—like flooring and labor for the Boutique; volunteers and donations for the "Adopt a Room" projects; and gifts of design, fashion, and presentation to help us accomplish our first step toward opening as the Hope Center.

First Giving Engine

The Redefined Hope Boutique opened for business in May of 2017. Rachel and Sarah started by reaching out to local churches and asking for clothing donations. Once they had a good amount of clothing, they created a social media following and put together their first sale on Facebook. They made $800 from this first sale. I was amazed—$800 from free clothing! They donated $400 to the Hope Center's general fund and reinvested the other $400. They did a few more sales, and each time they donated half of the money to the general fund and reinvested the rest. This is how they began making a small profit, even though they had started with $0. They were determined to reach their goal of paying the Hope Center's monthly lease payment of just over $10,000.

The Boutique's business began to grow, and so the business expanded and took over the entire lobby area of 5,000 square feet. The two rooms it first started in are now Cuppa Hope Coffee Shop. The Boutique puts on a spring and fall fashion show with volunteer models from the ages of 10 to 70. This provides a fun time for guests while also raising awareness of human trafficking and creating networking connections for the Center. The Boutique directors have created a unique in-store experience and keep working hard to run the store with a level of quality that inspires hope. One of the best things about the Boutique is that it now has created employment opportunities for our residents. This is a way to have jobs on campus for the residents, so they can learn life skills and hard work in such areas as fashion, design, retail, postage and handling, and presentation while earning an income. Rachel and Sarah enjoy the opportunity to invest in the lives of these ladies and their futures.

Even in the midst of the COVID pandemic, when many businesses have been closing their doors, the Boutique has opened two other locations. One is a storefront next to some popular restaurants and shops in Irvington, which is a historic community in Indianapolis. The other is a smaller version of the Boutique in a storefront building next to a historic restaurant, The Kopper Kettle, in Morristown, Indiana. God provided this building rent-free. Of course, He did! God has used Rachel and Sarah's heart of passion to make a difference to grow their business and this giving engine from the humble beginnings of their first $800 sale to where the sales for the year of 2021 were $925,000.

God is moving, and the ladies are accomplishing their goal of paying our monthly lease payment. But greater giving is on its way!

Waiting for God's provision or a need to be met can seem small in the scope of what God is really wanting to do in the lives of people. As a driven person with a classic type A personality, learning to wait upon the Lord has been a challenge but also a joy as I have seen Him bring forth His miracles and answers to prayer. I turned sixty-six this year, and it has taken me a lifetime to learn to wait patiently. So learn from me: Don't wait a lifetime to find out this wonderful truth about waiting, so you can see His favor through miracles and answers to prayer in your life too.

Promises to Read:

Philippians 4:6–8: "Do not be anxious about anything, but in every situation, by prayer and petition, with thanksgiving, present your requests to God. And the peace of God, which transcends all understanding, will guard your hearts and your minds in Christ Jesus. Finally, brothers and sisters, whatever is true, whatever is noble, whatever is right, whatever is pure, whatever is lovely, whatever is admirable, if anything is excellent or praiseworthy, think about such things."

Prayer to Pray:

Lord, help us to learn to wait upon you and allow You to guide and provide. Show us that waiting is not wasting time but using it to discern Your divine will. Always remind us that it is Your work, not ours, and we get to join You to accomplish great things. In Jesus' name, Amen.

I would like to conclude this chapter by including a written contribution by one of Hope Center Indy's graduates, which goes well with this chapter because she also shares about her experience of being an employee in the Boutique. Hope Center Indy took careful consideration in the collection and sharing of all resident stories contained in this book. All stories are shared with explicit and informed consent from the owners of those stories. See page 272 for more details.

Hope Center Graduate, Shena's Story (As Identified by the owner of this story)

I arrived at Hope Center Indy in August 2018. I had been drugged, trafficked, and exploited by people I had known and trusted. Thanks to a nurse at the last hospital I visited out of the many I went to over a six-month period, and thanks to the Indiana State Police, I found out about The Hope Center. When I got to The Hope Center, I was at the end of my rope. I had no hope left in humanity, no hope left in myself, and unfortunately, no hope left in God. I mean, after all, how can a good God allow such heinous and evil things to happen to a person?

What I didn't realize at the time was that God had never left me. He was with me through it all, but I was too angry, bitter, and resentful to see it. Like I said, when I got to the Hope Center, I was utterly and completely lost and hopeless. The Hope Center almost seemed too good to be true. These people provided me with a safe place to lay my head at night. It took months for the awful nightmares to subside (to this day, I still occasionally have them), but every time I'd wake up out of a dead sleep scared and afraid, I'd look around, remember where I was, and feel a strange sense of peace.

Things were different, I could feel it, but I couldn't make sense of it or begin to explain it.

I started attending daily Bible studies, weekly Celebrate Recovery meetings, church every Sunday, as well as various classes throughout the week (Bible class in which I studied my identity as a child of God, art classes, and physical activity/workout classes, to name a few). After I'd been there for a few months, I was given the opportunity to go work with the Boutique directors. Since I had developed somewhat of an anxiety problem and it was hard for me to be around large groups of people due to what I'd been through, I was given the opportunity to work by myself or sometimes with another Boutique employee or volunteer in the Hope Center's clothing donation room.

The constant influx of clothes, hygiene products, and multiple other items people donated blew me away. Here was a place that was full of godly, loving people who just wanted to help others who had been beaten down by life. Many people donated their time and energy, and the people who couldn't donate time by volunteering helped out in whatever way they could. I'd spend my days taking in donations and pulling out items that could be taken up to the resident boutique. (These people cared so much, they provided the residents with their own boutique to go shop in, free of charge. I never once wanted for anything during my two-year stay at the Hope Center).

On occasion and as needed, I'd go help out in the public boutique, Redefined Hope Boutique. Redefined Hope Boutique donates all proceeds back to the Hope Center to keep the lights on and pay the bills, so people like me have a place to go when it seems like all is lost, and they have no other option. The Boutique also has a coffee shop, and I was given the opportunity to learn how to make gourmet and specialty coffees. The Boutique has two fashion shows a year, and I was given the opportunity to be a part of that. Once again, I was amazed at how people showed up—not only to attend the fashion show, but also to shop for the benefit of the Hope Center. People were so happy to know that they were shopping for a cause that financially supports the Center and helps those in need.

The people who volunteered at the Center while I was there and all who came to shop and/or donate were always so kind, supportive, and encouraging to me that I couldn't help but see God at work. Never before have I been so blessed to be a part of something as great as the Hope Center. (Not to mention, they paid me to work in the Boutique, as well, which they didn't need to do, but they did anyway.) These people loved me at a time when I couldn't love myself. They helped me back up onto my feet and showed me God's love in such a real and tangible way that it literally changed my life in every single way: How I see God, how I see myself, and how I see others!

I moved out of the Hope Center in September 2020, and got an apartment. I still struggle sometimes because life in general is hard, and it's not easy to live a life that is wholly dedicated to God when the world is so very the opposite. But I would rather live my life with God than without because I have seen both sides. I owe my life to God and thank Jesus every day for His unconditional love, sacrifice, and forgiveness of my sins. Had I not found Jesus at the time in my life when I did with the help of the Hope Center, I can honestly say I don't know where I would be.

I am so grateful for all the people who have been a part of the Hope Center, who took and continue to take the time to help broken and lost people slowly but surely put their lives back together. It is such a blessing when someone is an active and real example of the hands and feet of Jesus. Giving to others in need is not easy, but Pastor Nolen, his family, and all volunteers and staff members have truly blessed my life and shown me the love of Jesus that I had never seen before and will never forget. Thank you, Hope Center volunteers and staff, for making a difference in the world and for being part of the change you want to see.

Redefined Hope Boutique

Redefined Hope Boutique

Redefined Hope Boutique

Coffee Shop

8

$10,000 Reasons to Praise the Lord

Along the way, we have witnessed God do small and big miracles for Hope Center Indy. As we have worked to build this ministry, we have been responsible for paying the utility bills for this huge campus (which could take your breath away!), the maintenance needs (the campus was almost seventy years old!), as well as staff salaries. The financial needs are significant, but God has shown us that He is a trustworthy provider.

I realized it would be a big task to raise funds for the Hope Center. I was freed up from taking a salary from the Hope Center because my church, Brookville Road Community Church (BRCC), where I had pastored for thirty-three years, committed to continue paying my salary for a few years to help the Hope Center ministry get going. This was decided by the board of elders and the generous congregation as they helped us get the Hope Center ministry off the ground.

This gift of receiving my salary from BRCC was especially a blessing because by 2018, the Hope Center had around ten full-time employees working in the ministry. At this time, we were providing 24/7 care, 365 days a year for the residents in our program. We needed to make sure we could fully fund a staff to handle this responsibility. (My daughter Sara was one of our staff members to help found our program. For four years, she lived in one of the staff apartments and served along the other program staff to minister to our residents. Sara is also an attorney, so she was able to assist our residents with legal needs and often take them to any local court dates they may have had.)

God was working behind the scenes to orchestrate His wonderful plan. God was going to get our attention by using the number 10,000. The first time the Hope Center received a gift for $10,000 was in the spring of 2018. In my prayer journal entry for April 8, 2018, I thanked God for a $10,000 gift designated for the purchase of a vehicle for the transportation of the residents. Then, over the next several months, I began to notice we were receiving more checks for $10,000.

It dawned on me that God was doing something with gifts of $10,000. Because I saw this pattern, I decided to research what the Bible says about the number of 10,000. As I mentioned, I enjoy numerology, the study of numbers in the Bible.

The number *ten* means "completeness." The number *thousand* means "immensity, fullness of quantity." For example, in Psalm 50:10, we read, *"For every beast of the forest is mine and cattle upon a thousand hills."* Now we all know there are more than a thousand hills on earth. This passage implies that God owns all the cattle on all the hills. It shows the immensity of His ownership. He owns it all— everything, everywhere. So if we put the meaning of *ten* and of *thousand* together, we get the complete, immense, full quantity of God. So, 10,000 could very well reveal God's complete and full provision for the Hope Center.

In November of 2018, I was walking down the hallway at the Hope Center, and our treasurer, Holly, said, "Pastor, payroll is due Friday, and it must be in our account tomorrow to be processed." She didn't need to say anymore. I knew what she meant: Our bank account did not have the required balance to meet the payroll.

I was leaving for an appointment, and on my way, I prayed, "Lord, Your payroll is due tomorrow, so what are You going to do about that?" After all, this is His ministry. After my appointment, I headed back to the Center. I must confess—I am not proud of it—but I started playing God with a small "g." I started thinking about what my wife, Tonia, and I could give and who I could call to ask for funds to meet the payroll. I know that as a leader, my leadership skills wanted to kick in and make things happen.

When I arrived back at the Hope Center, Sara, our development director, met me in the hallway with an envelope. She said, "A gentleman called and wanted to make sure he had put his check in the mailed envelope. I checked for him that he had, and I let him know."

I thanked her, went into my office, picked up the envelope he had mailed us, and pulled out a check—it was for $10,000. This was enough to make up the difference for payroll! Earlier, when I was on my way to the appointment, I told the Lord His payroll was due and asked Him what He was going to do about it.

God probably said, "Hubert, did you check your mail today? It's already there."

On this day I had $10,000 reasons to praise the Lord for His kindness, goodness, and His provision for our staff who were being paid on time.

On Friday of the same week, I went to the mailbox, and there was another envelope from the gentleman who had just sent us the check for $10,000. I opened it and inside was another check for $10,000. I thought, "Oh, my! Maybe he didn't remember that he had just sent the first check." So, I asked my son David to email this gentleman and ask him if he had intended to mail us a second check. If it was not his intention to give us another check, we would return the check to him. Within a couple of hours, he emailed us back. Quoting from James 1:17, his returned email read, "All good and perfect gifts come from above." Dave and I looked at each other, thinking, *Wow*! We rejoiced over this double portion of not just one, but two $10,000 gifts.

The Favor of $10,000

This same week, the Youth Opportunity Foundation was having a Gala on Human Trafficking. They reached out to me and asked if I would speak and also if one of our residents would share their story. When we arrived at the red-carpet affair, they had a makeup artist there to do all our residents' makeup. They were treated like royalty. At this banquet table, they served hors d'oeuvres and a wonderful steak dinner.

Other people were being served wine with their dinner. The residents asked me, "Pastor, can we have a glass of wine?"

Most of our residents deal with addictions, and they are working hard to maintain their sobriety. A glass of wine would definitely not fit into their recovery plan. The other Hope Center staff members and I smiled at them and said, "No."

They smiled. They were just hoping.

After everyone was served dinner, one of our graduates, Megan, was invited to the front to speak. As Megan spoke, the people were so moved. (Read Megan's story at the end of this chapter!) The founder of the organization stood up and said, "Let's receive some money in Megan's honor to be given as college scholarships."

You know how much they raised? $10,000! So, ten $1,000 scholarships would be given in her name, and she would be the first $1,000 recipient to use toward her college education.

Only a week later, I saw God do something again with the number $10,000. As a longtime board member, I attended the board meeting of World Renewal International, which is a missionary organization with missionaries in fifty countries. Over the thirty-five years of serving, they have put their missionaries and field projects first and the organization's needs second. Praying and hoping they could meet their annual budget for 2018 was no different. After hearing field reports from missionaries, the board focused on World Renewal International's $20,000 shortfall for the year.

As we discussed the need, my heart longed to pray over Gary, the president of the organization. I wanted to ask God to give World Renewal the same favor of $10,000 gifts we were receiving at the Hope Center. I didn't want to keep this special gift of favor quietly to myself. If I would share this favor with others, surely God would do even more. The $10,000 favor wasn't just for the Hope Center; it was for other people who had faith to believe God could do the very same thing for their ministries.

At the end of the meeting, I told the other board members the stories of the $10,000 checks the Hope Center had received recently. I told them I wanted to pray for Gary, the president of the organization to receive this blessing for World Renewal. The others agreed, so we gathered around Gary and prayed in faith that God would give this ministry the favor of $10,000. This was on a Thursday, and on Saturday, I got a text from Gary, saying that he had received a check for $10,000! I was so excited for him and praised our Lord. The next Saturday I received another text from Gary, and he said World Renewal had received an additional $10,000 check. I called Gary, and he shared that one of the missionaries who was present at that meeting when we prayed had also received a $10,000 gift. As I drove home that evening, I rejoiced in our Lord's goodness and kindness in showing His favor.

As I started to share this testimony of $10,000 gifts, others wanted me to pray over them too—of course, who wouldn't? One thing I noticed quickly: It didn't translate to individuals but only to ministries and not to all ministries, at least not right away.

In the first week of January 2019, a ministry asked if I would pray for their ministry to receive this favor. I prayed for God's favor and provision for their ministry. During this prayer time, I also asked God if He would keep this $10,000 favor going for the Hope Center and further into 2019. David told me that he wrote in his prayer journal that he asked God to provide the Hope Center with 100 gifts of $10,000. I told him that I liked his faith! So, we started praying together that God would bless the Hope Center with 100 gifts of $10,000.

I had a meeting at a local coffee shop that same day to give a couple an update on what was happening at the Center. After a half hour, the man took out his billfold and pulled out a check he had already written for $10,000.

I looked at the check in amazement. I said, "Do you know what God is doing with $10,000 checks at the Hope Center?"

They said, "No, what?"

So I explained to them about the $10,000 gifts that God was giving to the ministry. Their eyes filled with tears because they had listened to God and written just the God-appointed amount on their check.

The Favor Continues

Before I started Hope Center Indy, I received Isaiah 45:3 as a promise: "I will give you hidden treasures, riches stored in secret places, so that you may know that I am the Lord the God of Israel, who summons you by name."

I used to think this promise had something to do with my personal finances (which could have used some hidden treasures and stored riches), but now I know this promise given over ten years ago was for the provision of the Hope Center Indy. Over the last couple of years, God has given so many hidden treasures and stored riches, it has caused my heart to rejoice and proclaim His goodness. It has caused my faith to grow. My faith muscle has been worked out and enlarged to believe Him for more.

I love to share the story of the time when David was working on fixing some issues with the IT equipment at the Hope Center. He was feeling frustrated because he wasn't trained in IT, but he was trying his best to help since we didn't have anyone else helping with IT at the time. David's cell phone number was listed as a contact number for the Hope Center, and someone called his phone. He answered the call, and it was a man who said he was from an insurance company. Because David was focused on fixing the IT problem, he told the insurance agent, "I'm sorry, but I'm not interested in buying any insurance right now," and he hung up the phone. His phone rang again, and David saw the caller ID was the same number. He answered politely as the insurance agent introduced himself again. David told him again that he was not interested in buying any insurance today and then hung up again.

The insurance agent called back a third time, and before David could say anything else, the insurance agent said, "Our company would like to donate money to the Hope Center."

David then apologized for hanging up on him and thanked him for wanting to donate. That insurance company ended up giving a $10,000 gift to the Hope Center. I often joke that Dave is the only guy I know that hung up not once, but twice on a $10,000 gift.

One day a lady came into the Boutique and handed me an envelope. I took it into my office and sat down in my chair to open it. Inside it was a check for $50,000. I went back out to see if she was still in the Boutique, and she was. I said to her, "I had no idea how great a gift you had given me. I want to thank you and your husband for your generosity."

She looked at me, smiled, and said, "We were going to give you five $10,000 checks, but we wanted to enlarge your faith to believe and start a new level of blessing."

Wow, I thought I was doing well believing God for all these $10,000 gifts. Now she wants me to go to a new level of faith. I am all in! I realized God can do so much and provide in ways I can't imagine. Between April 2018 and August 2022, we have received 88 gifts of $10,000 and 3 gifts of $50,000! This is so close to David's original prayer for 100 gifts of $10,000! God has shown His ability to provide, and I'm excited to see how God will continue to provide. The reality is that without these $10,000 gifts, it would be impossible for us to maintain the operating expenses and grow the ministry of the Hope Center.

I always want people to know that God's generous provision for the Hope Center is because of God's heart for the women who are its residents. We know that God's heart for them is that they will come to know His love and transforming power to heal. His provision of all these $10,000 checks is His way of saying, "I love you, and I have a plan for your life."

I want our Hope Center team to always remember to worship God for being our great Provider and to remember and thank Him for the gifts He gives us. Perhaps you have heard one of my all-time favorite worship songs, "10,000 Reasons," which was written by Matt Redman and Jonas Myrin. Mr. Redman shares that the song was based on the opening of Psalm 103. He mentions that the song reiterates how "we live beneath an unceasing flow of goodness, kindness, greatness, and holiness, and every day we're given reason after reason why Jesus is so completely and utterly worthy of our highest and best devotion."[viii] I thought of this song often when we would see the $10,000-gifts come in for the Hope Center, and I would thank God for giving us 10,000 reasons to praise Him!

Humbled by Sacrifice 10,000 Ways

When I tell these stories about people who gave the gift of $10,000, it can be easy for some people to think that all these generous givers had plenty of money to give away. But that is not the case. I realized for so many, their gift was a major sacrifice for them and family, business, or church. Time and again, I was so humbled by these sacrifices to give to the Hope Center ministry. One such moment stands out. I was invited to speak at a local church in the Indianapolis area, so Tonia and I and a few other people from the Hope Center joined them one Sunday morning. This was a church plant that had purchased land and built their first building. The building was a small 2,000-square-foot fellowship hall, but it accommodated their congregation. In the service, I shared about the Hope Center and how God was blessing the ministry. I told some of the stories about the $10,000 gifts.

After the service, I prayed for some of the people in the congregation. After I had finished, the pastor came up to me and said, "I'm so sorry, but I forgot to take up an offering for the Hope Center. But the elders are discussing what we would like to give as a gift now."

I reassured him no offering or gift was necessary. I had come to their church that morning to share what God was doing.

After everyone had left, the pastor handed me an envelope and thanked us for coming. Once in our vehicle, I opened the envelope, and inside was a check. I unfolded the check, and what I saw literally took my breath away: a check for $10,000! I could hardly believe my eyes. This small congregation with high hopes of building a new sanctuary in the future had just given this enormous gift. I was totally caught off guard. I didn't know what to think. Being a former church planter, I know how hard it is to raise money for a new sanctuary. I was humbled by the generosity of these few, but faith-filled believers.

The next day I was going to call the pastor and tell him that I didn't even know if I should accept such a great gift on your part. I wanted to say, "I can't receive this. Please, Pastor, keep this for your church and the vision you have to reach your community with the hope of Christ." But while I was preparing for my conversation with him, I felt our Lord say to me, *Don't deprive my people of this blessing to give and be part of what I'm doing at the Hope Center.*

I realized this was not my decision but God's. He was moving in their hearts to bless the Center, and in turn, He would bless this church for their faithfulness. I called the pastor and told him how humbled I was and how hard it was for me to receive their faith-filled gift. I also told him about what I felt the Lord shared with me about His desire to bless the church for blessing the Hope Center. The pastor was excited to bless us and to see what God would do for their church.

As I was wrote this chapter, I called the church to follow up. The church told me that God did bless them with gifts of $10,000 and $20,000 after they gave their offering to the Hope Center! I think it is great that God gave them their gift plus two more for their sacrifice. At times, we must have faith that our sacrifice is not a sacrifice at all. Our sacrifice becomes God's channel where He is able to bless us even more, sometimes $10,000 times more.

I don't know what you are asking God to provide—maybe a $10,000 gift would be a good start. But just remember that He is able to meet all of your needs according to His glorious riches in Christ Jesus. Maybe you should also keep a list of the ways God answers your prayers and provides for your needs. You might be surprised by the 10,000 different ways He is faithful to you.

Promises to Read:

Psalm 103:1–2: "Praise the Lord, O my soul; all my inmost being praise His holy name. Praise the Lord, O my soul, and forget not all his benefits."

Philippians 4:19: "And my God will meet all your needs according to his glorious riches in Christ Jesus."

Jeremiah 29:11: "'For I know the plans I have for you,' declares the Lord, 'plans to prosper you and not to harm you, plans to give you hope and a future.'"

James 1:17: "Every good and perfect gift is from above, coming down from the Father of the heavenly lights."

Prayer to Pray:

Jesus, I know You are the Great Provider! Help me to seek Your will, and help me experience Your divine favor and blessing. I ask that the divine favor You have given to the Hope Center would be given to ministries and others who so desperately need to see Your mighty hand of provision. In Your name, Amen.

I would like to conclude this chapter by including a written contribution by one of Hope Center Indy's graduates. Hope Center Indy took careful consideration in the collection and sharing of all resident stories contained in this book. All stories are shared with explicit and informed consent from the owners of those stories. See page 272 for details.

Megan's Story (As Identified by the owner of this story):

Growing up, I had a baseball team of seven siblings. My dad worked hard and long hours, my mom drank, and I was mommy Jr., taking care of my siblings because I was the oldest. Eventually having all of us kids became too much for my mom, and she dropped us off with my dad when I was nine. We would hear from her here and there.

When I was ten, my dad had a girlfriend, and his girlfriend's son molested me. By age eleven I was drinking. After that I slowly started on a downward spiral, and getting drunk became a regular thing in my teens. At eighteen I started smoking marijuana. Soon thereafter I was into Xanax and pain pills. By the age of twenty, I was strung out on cocaine, and crack followed close behind. These things led me to a man I met when I was twenty-three. I thought he loved me—only in the end, he tore me down and manipulated me. The mind games he played, the physical and mental abuse—it broke me down. He used me to fund his lifestyle.

Around this time my mom came back into my life. It was a relationship of using together, but I did not care because all I had ever wanted was my momma. At the age of twenty-

155

four, I became an I.V. drug user, and heroin became a close friend.

Over all this time, I had overdosed three times, been in and out of drug treatments, jails, baker-act facilities, and I had nothing to do with my family. A few years ago, my mother lost her battle with addiction, which threw me into a tailspin. Months after losing my mother, I ended up in the hospital with endocarditis, a blood clot in my heart (from I.V. drug use) and pneumonia (from being homeless in seventeen-degree weather). My kidneys were failing, I couldn't even walk because the infection was attacking the muscle tissue in my legs. My body was shutting down on me, and the doctors were talking about open-heart surgery if we couldn't get rid of the infection.

I remember lying in that hospital bed, praying for help. I was scared and angry! I did not want to die like my mother had. After nine weeks in the hospital, I got better. I would like to say that I learned my lesson, but the truth is I went right back to the streets, to taking drugs, and to trafficking myself. This was all I knew. I was homeless, sleeping behind a dumpster, doing the same old thing again. After that I came to a point of contemplating suicide. I stood on the side of US Highway 1, staring at all the cars passing by, and wanting to end my life. I was going to step out into traffic. I had had enough, and I was tired!

Suddenly, a woman came out of nowhere. She walked over to me and asked if I was okay. I was honest with her and told her that I wasn't okay. She called 911, and an ambulance came to pick me up. As I was getting into the ambulance, I turned to thank her, and she was nowhere to be found. Maybe she was God's angel on a mission, at least for me she was.

I first began my new journey toward healing at a program for women in my home state for a year and a half, and then I came to Hope Center Indy. The Lord began a good work in me, and I became a new person in Christ. The Lord has restored my family relationships, especially with my dad and stepmom. I have received inner healing for my anger and abandonment issues towards my mother. I learned to love myself, and that it's okay not to be okay all the time. Most importantly, I have a relationship with my heavenly Father that can never be broken, and I am forever changed because of Him.

Father God reminds me daily that my past does not define me and that I have hope for my future. The past couple of years have been scary but so much fun! I paid off a substantial debt that hurt my credit and prevented me from getting my license. I recently celebrated my third anniversary, and I can for once say that I am in a healthy and stable relationship. I've also successfully held a job for longer than two years and continued my education. I have

157

four classes left before I graduate with my associate degree. I will then be attending classes for sign language because I wish to be a sign language interpreter. It has not been easy by any means, but I was able to stay strong with Him guiding me.

I believe God led me to the Hope Center for such a time as this. I am a transformed woman because of the Lord. If you would have met me a few years ago and then seen me now, you would easily see this new person Christ has made and is continuing to change. Have I arrived? No, but I am well on my way. I no longer see that pitiful, failure junkie when I look in the mirror. Now I see a strong, courageous woman of God.

I will soon celebrate six years sober! Six years without heroin, six years without crack, six years without meth, and six years without a needle. I never thought it was possible for me to get clean, let alone become a productive member of society. I will continue to share my story in hopes of helping others. We do recover! To Him be all the glory, honor, and praise.

9

Take Heart Residential

At the Hope Center main entrance, a candle sits on the counter. A note next to the candle reads, "When the candle is lit, please pray. We have a new resident on her way!" Usually, our intake director is in contact with a potential resident at least a week before she comes to our program. Once we know that she has committed to coming, we turn on the electric candle for the few days before she arrives. We realize this is a big step for this lady to take in her healing journey, and we want to pray for her in this vulnerable time of making the transition to our campus.

It takes tremendous courage for the women to come to a new place and commit to a long-term restorative program. That is why we ask people to join us in praying, especially for new residents. Our staff members know that the women may be feeling anxiety, hopelessness, and any number of challenging emotions when they walk onto our campus. Our staff recently renamed our program "Take Heart Residential." This phrase "Take Heart" comes from multiple verses in the Bible that inspire us to know that even in the dark storms of life, Jesus tells us to take heart and have courage because He is with us. He gives hope to see us through that dark time to a brighter future. Our staff especially love the story in Matthew 9 of the woman suffering from a blood disease who perseveres to make her way to Jesus. This woman believes that if she can touch the hem of His cloak, she will be healed. Then it says in Matthew 9:22, "Jesus turned and saw her. 'Take heart, daughter,' he said, 'your faith has healed you.' And the woman was healed at that moment." This truth speaks hope into our troubled days. We want to encourage our residents to reach out to Jesus just like the woman did in Matthew 9 because we believe that Jesus wants to embrace them as His daughters and bring healing into their lives.

Another bible verse that uses the phrase "take heart" is John 16:33, when Jesus says to his disciples, "In this world you will have trouble. But take heart! I have overcome the world." We also find this phrase in Psalm 31:24: "Be strong and take heart, all you who hope in the Lord." Our staff works daily to remind our residents that they are loved by God and can be overcomers through Christ. Gina Colclazier, our Director of Residential Ministries, has said, "It is a beautiful thing to watch as our residents grasp hold of the truth that through Christ they can be overcomers! As they gain new insights and spiritual strength, we get to see glimmers of them beginning to grow past their trauma and pain, revealing signs of new hope and a transformed life."

Our Residential Program

As we were getting started in 2016 and 2017, David and I went to several conferences on serving survivors of sex trafficking. We also hosted staff trainings on trauma by experts on our campus. We asked ourselves, "What would it take for these ladies to take steps forward? What things do we want these ladies to walk away with when they complete our program? How can we equip them to be successful?"

We decided early in the process that our program would be for women eighteen years old and older. We realized that it was a long process to get licensed to run a residential program for minors, so we made the decision to specialize in helping adult women.

As we did our research, we realized that every survivor of human trafficking is unique. Every survivor is going to have unique strengths and unique challenges to overcome. This is why each resident in our program has a case manager to address her needs and goals.

As we continued praying and brainstorming with other leaders, we knew that we wanted our program to have a college feel, where the women could take classes that would help them move forward in life. After much thought and research, we chose five pillars to base our program around:

1. Spirituality
2. Wellness
3. Career & Education
4. Financial Literacy
5. Relational Health

Even before we ever had any residents, we began sharing our plan for the five pillars with our Hope Center supporters. My role at the Center has always been to be the visionary instead of the person who is implementing the vision on a day-to-day basis. So, as we began to hire program staff, which included a program director, case managers, and res techs (short for resident technicians) who would be with the residents throughout their daily schedule, we cast the vision of the five pillars to them. The female program staff would be working with the women daily, so we wanted them to be excited about this vision. The five pillars became what we called our "Plan of Hope." They are designed to help each lady grow in the areas of spirituality, wellness, career and education, financial literacy, and relational health in a fifteen-month program.

Our residential program opened in August of 2017. Between 2017 and now (2022), we have had some wonderful program staff and leaders bring their strengths and expertise to help us continue to develop our program. We have realized that providing residential care for survivors of trafficking is an emerging field, and we are committed to going deeper in our understanding of how to best serve this specific population. In 2021, Hope Center Indy was accepted into The Samaritan Women Institute for Shelter Care mentorship program. Through our partnership with this institute, we have spent time learning from the nation's top experts in this field, so we continue to grow in our staff training that is specific to serving women who are overcoming sex trafficking and sexual exploitation.

Each quarter the residents take at least one class in each of the five pillars. We have five phases for the residents to work through.

Our Spiritual Pillar

I have been a pastor for forty-five years, and evangelism and discipleship will always be at the heart of who I am. Our Hope Center team also prioritizes evangelism and discipleship. They are among our top goals as we provide holistic care to meet the residents' practical needs. This is why we are upfront about telling people that we are a Christ-centered campus.

All the women who decide to come into our program know upfront that we are a Christ-centered program. Most of the women who come into our program already have an awareness of God and want to know if He can help them. Maybe their grandmother or another relative took them to church when they were young. Or maybe at some point in their lives another Christian helped them and prayed with them, and now they want to understand God better. We recognize that there are other women who come into our program who are not as interested in the spiritual side of things, and we understand that. When they sign up for the program, they know they do not ever have to do things like pray out loud if they don't want to, but they do need to be respectful of our faith. We know that every person is at a different point in their life journey, and we pray that God will reveal His truth to them and help them come to faith in Christ.

As mentioned previously in this book, we have a Prayer Center on our campus that serves as our place to have a weekly Wednesday evening prayer and worship service together with our residents, staff, and volunteers who are on shift. One of the things I often share is that I want our residents to learn to sincerely connect with God through prayer. Even though our program is fifteen months long, the women are free to choose to leave early if they want to. We never know when a resident may leave and what situation she may be going back into, but if we can introduce her to Jesus and teach her to pray, then we know that she can call on Jesus wherever she goes.

In addition to our weekly prayer and worship service, the residents have daily devotions every morning, go to church on Sundays, and also have the opportunity to study the Bible in some of their other weekly classes.

Our Wellness Pillar

Our Wellness pillar covers the categories of trauma counseling, addiction recovery, physical health, and therapeutic and expressive arts. We partner with other clinical organizations like a clinical counseling center, substance abuse IOP (intensive outpatient programs), our local community health center, and a mental health and recovery center run by one of our church partners. It is a joy for our staff to celebrate milestones of sobriety with the residents and other big and small victories of overcoming the trauma they have endured.

It is important for our program to address the physical needs the women coming into our program may have. We have a good partnership with the community health center in our area that we take our residents to for physical health assessments. Often, when women have been trafficked, and especially if they have been abusing drugs and alcohol, their physical health has been neglected. We want to address any physical health needs they may have with the support of trusted doctors. We also have found that many of our residents need to address their dental health, and it's a priority for us to take them to all their dental appointments.

Our Career and Education Pillar

Many women who come into our program (we estimate a little less than half of them) do not have a high school diploma. We have an educational director who works with each resident's case manager to do an educational assessment for her. Based on this assessment, the resident begins taking classes on our campus to work toward completing her high school equivalency exam. We are thankful for our educational director and volunteers who spend their time each week helping our residents progress in their math, reading, and writing skills, etc. Even if a resident doesn't stay long enough or isn't able to pass the high school equivalency exam, that resident is usually able to improve her reading level from a third- or fourth-grade reading level to a high school reading level. This is something we are excited about because we know this helps the resident improve her confidence and equips her to read and research things important to her independence.

Our educational director also provides a digital literacy class the women can take to give them certification in

Microsoft Word. They can add this to their resume to show potential employers that they have these particular computer skills. Our education director can also discuss other certification programs the residents may be interested in and help them get started—whether it be hospitality, culinary arts, etc. He also can help them explore other college options to see if they want to start taking any online college classes.

We are very excited about our growing ability to offer residents on-campus internships and jobs. Usually, about six to eight months into her programming (depending on her goals and progress), she can start working in her on-campus job. Our businesses on campus are eager to help provide gainful employment for residents who choose to apply to work for them. This can allow the women to work in a healthy environment that is supportive of their life goals, especially when it comes to maintaining sobriety. The women have often said that it is hard to work in other places because of how many other employees or customers are using drugs or alcohol on the property, and it becomes a temptation for them.

We also have connected with a few companies that have remote job opportunities for our residents. These companies have job opportunities that can be done on the computer and phone. Often the residents will have an office space on our campus while they work at this job, but they can continue in this job when they move out. We have had great success with these companies employing our residents and graduates. We are continuing to find good job opportunities for the women because secure, gainful employment is foundational for them as they move forward in their lives.

Our Financial Pillar

We realize that for our residents to go out and be successful, they will need to learn to budget their money and be able to support themselves financially after they leave our campus. As the residents begin their programming, they work with their case manager to set up a checking and savings account. We have partnered with ministry leaders to teach them a financial literacy class each week. After the residents have reached the point in their programming where they have started working at a job, they can get advice from their financial mentors on how to budget their money and begin saving for their next steps. Part of their last phase in our program includes them finding transportation, a place to live, and having at least three months' rent saved up. At times, we have had cars donated to the Hope Center that we can then gift to our residents after they graduate from our program.

Soon after we started the Hope Center, we realized we had to have a transitional program on campus for some of our women to move into after they graduated. Many of the women do not have a strong support system to return to after graduation. Some women can be very nervous about starting somewhere else if they don't have a strong support system in place. This led us to begin our transitional program called Hope Community on our campus. Because we have the space, we were able to dedicate a whole floor to our Hope Community residents. In this program, they have independence and are integrating back into society. They are able to stay in the program for two more years if they choose. The women living in Hope Community work full-time jobs and pay rent for the private bedroom and bathroom they occupy. This helps them to set their budget and build their credit history. Our Hope Community staff still holds them accountable for maintaining a sober living environment by administering random drug tests and holding regular mentoring meetings to help them stay on track with their life goals. Often the Hope Community residents come to Wednesday prayer meetings to join with everyone else every week.

Our Relational Pillar

Our team has the desire to help our residents learn what it means to have healthy family relationships, healthy friendships, healthy support systems, and healthy dating/marriage relationships. As mentioned earlier in this book, many survivors of sex trafficking have experienced challenging childhoods in their families growing up that may have included substance abuse, poverty, violence, abuse, or neglect in the home. Now, living in a sober community, the residents learn communication and conflict resolution skills during their everyday lives with the other residents. We are intentional about connecting the residents with a mentor and a sponsor if they so choose, and these can become important relationships that support them.

Most of the residents in our program have children, but many have been separated from their children for a long time. Often the children are living with another relative or a foster parent. We are able to give the residents the chance to have family visits on our campus. During the family visitation times, the residents can reconnect with their children and other positive family members. One of the biggest blessings we have seen with our residents is how they have been able to reconnect with their previously estranged children and other family members.

To Learn More

I have given a very brief overview of our residential program in this chapter. If you would like to learn more, I encourage you to go to hopecenterindy.org and search for our latest blogs, videos, podcasts, and updates about our residential programming. In those updates, you can hear more from our female program leaders who are working with the residents on a regular basis.

Our goal is to continue growing our program until we reach full capacity on our large campus. We know that God has been faithful to bring the leaders, resources, and partnerships we have needed thus far, and He will continue to be faithful to bring everything that is needed to grow our program in the years to come. We would like to end this chapter by sharing two more essays from Hope Center graduates. We hope you will see that there is a need for the Hope Center to work hard to provide a refuge for women to heal and rebuild their lives, and we hope you will celebrate what God has done in their lives with us.

Promises to Read:

Psalm 31:24: "Be strong and take heart, all you who hope in the Lord."

Matthew 9:22: "Jesus turned and saw her. 'Take heart, daughter,' he said, 'your faith has healed you.' And the woman was healed at that moment."

John 16:33: "In this world you will have trouble. But take heart! I have overcome the world."

Prayer to Pray:

Jesus, I pray for the survivors of sex trafficking and organizations like Hope Center Indy that are working hard to support them on their healing journeys. Please meet the survivors' needs and encourage them as they take steps forward in their lives. Give them a hope and a future in You. In Jesus' name, Amen

---

Hope Center Indy took careful consideration in the collection and sharing of all resident stories contained in this book. All stories are shared with explicit and informed consent from the owners of those stories. See page 272 for more details.

Tiffany's Story (As Identified by the owner of this story)

I come from a large family, and I also have two children. Growing up was rough. I was a product of physical abuse, neglect, and molestation. My daddy left when I was two, and my mom tried to take care of eight kids by herself. I was in the foster care system for over ten years. After returning home, my mom married my stepfather and had two more kids. He was as crazy as they come, and they had big fights all the time. He would beat her; she would boil water and throw it on him. My aunt would take us to the park, but when we would come home, the house was a disaster.

Eventually they divorced, but he kept custody of the kids because my mom was on welfare. My mom broke down and stayed in bed for years.

From then, it was clear that we were on our own. I was molested by a neighbor when I was nine. I would have told my mom, but I watched her beat my sister for getting pregnant at thirteen. Mom was a religious fanatic. The only time she got out of bed was to go to church. Mom went to jail twice for the way she beat us. I didn't feel sorry for her because I always had a feeling that she liked beating us.

I bounced from foster home to foster home and from one group home to another. I was a habitual runaway at twelve. I thought I was so slick because I would stay on the run all summer and turn myself in so I could go to school. I met a man twenty years older than me and had my baby at sixteen. The crazy thing is, I graduated early and became the first in my family to graduate from high school at all, especially with a baby. I was emancipated when I turned 18 and moved away to study social work a year later.

I felt confused and angry about so many things, but I didn't know how to use my voice to say what I needed to say. Drinking became the center of my universe when I found out that it gave me a voice. And that is how I functioned. Everyone knew I was an alcoholic in the making, but I didn't care. Nothing made sense without a drink. I started dating a wide range of men. I wanted to be loved so much that I would say yes when my boyfriend asked me to do things I would be ashamed of doing. But it didn't occur to me to say no because I loved him, he took very good care of me, and I didn't want to be alone. Until one day, he became abusive after I told him I did not want to do something. After the first time he hit me, something changed, but I had to anyway.

I later met my husband, and we had a child together, though they never met each other. We broke up because we were too young to have gotten married. We struggled with our own demons. His family wanted to adopt my baby when I gave birth. They said if I let them have the baby, they would care for everything, but I would not be allowed to be part of my child's life. I declined.

I started nursing school when my baby was a year old. My family-in-law made me feel like trash, so I worked hard to graduate and get my license. This was the first time I got sober by sheer will--the first time I had gotten sober, period. It changed my life. I was self-reliant and had accomplished everything by myself. But the problem with self-reliance is, who do you turn to when your bottom falls out from under you?

I became a workaholic and did not have the energy to be a mother to my kids. I became moody and restless. During this time, I started using cocaine. It was a nightmare. It seemed like every guy I dated was abusive, and the fights started getting serious. No matter how much I gave or what

I did to make it work (which was anything because I had no boundaries), it didn't work. I knew that if I didn't get away soon, I would be killed.

Someone called the police one day, and they took my kids because the house was filthy, and I was drunk. I was a wreck. My addiction spiraled out of control. I was getting fired from jobs for calling in all the time. I was evicted from my apartment and started staying in motels, but I was also evicted because I passed out with drugs in the room. I was in ICU on my birthday due to liver failure. I missed my children, but I was knee-deep in my addiction and couldn't get sober long enough to visit them or comply with CPS. I was so overwhelmed that I gave up my youngest for adoption and sent the oldest to live with family. I decided to move out of state. I got clean and sober for 18 months until I relapsed. I lost control of who I became when I drank. I hit rock bottom, and I wanted to die. Drugs and alcohol were not working so I thought my life was over. But just because if feels like it's over, it doesn't mean it is.

When I came back to Indiana, I stopped by a local recovery program on my way to see someone. I was discharged from there after completing a thirty-day inpatient recovery program before, so they were familiar with me. I wanted to apply into their program again. They told me to come back in five days, when they would discharge current clients and admit new ones. I sat on my hands for five days. I was so excited because I had a flicker of hope. I was accepted into their program and completed another thirty-day inpatient program. However, this time, instead of sending me back to the streets, my case manager told me about Hope Center Indy. She didn't know much about it because she had never sent anyone there before and said I would be the first. A case manager from Hope Center Indy came to interview me. After the interview, she told me that I had been accepted. She may as well have said that I had just won a million dollars. I knew God was saying, "I heard your cries for help. I have a place for you. They will help you, but you have to do the work. I will be with you, but it's up to you to succeed."

Hope Center Indy is unlike any other place I've ever been to, and I've been to a few places. The staff and volunteers are unlike any other people I have ever met, and I've met a few people. Hope Center Indy provided me with a clean, safe shelter, food, and nice clothing. I was difficult and mistrusting, but that was okay. They showered me with grace. I found out that I had never met anyone who shows you what a faithful Christian looks like without saying a word. I can't express how much this place has changed me. I'm trusting people again. God is real and personal to me. My heart was crushed when my father died, but the staff and volunteers were there for me. I now have a relationship with my kids, after years of not even talking to them. While in the program, I had a stroke on my cerebellum, which controls balance only, so I have no cognitive or physical impairments at all! Hope Center Indy provided me with gainful employment, and as a result, I was able to enroll in a program for professionals overcoming addictions. I am now a graduate of the Take Heart Residential Program and licensed to practice nursing again. My God loved me back from despair. I am now thriving and excited to share my testimony of victory with the world.

Title: "Someone Like Sarah" (As Identified by the owner of this story)

As a young child, I lost my father, experienced abuse, and was removed from my mother's home because of her substance abuse. At the age of twelve, after twenty-two calls to child protective services, I was removed from my grandparents' home and placed into group homes until I turned eighteen. I thrived there, emotionally and physically. However, spiritually I was lost. I had experienced such a bad example of God's love through one of my relatives who had a mental illness. I thought if a servant of God could cause me so much pain and heartache, then I didn't want to serve that kind of God. I did not have any idea how love was supposed to feel. I did know that the type of love I had received in life so far was not the love I wanted. Like most

177

human beings, I started seeking this elusive thing in all the wrong places. I started hanging out with the wrong people.

I found the wrong kind of love. You see, my brain was already programmed to protect itself from things that most people would walk away from. At the age of eighteen, I found drugs. All of a sudden, love was irrelevant. All my emotions were numb in a short amount of time. I vividly remember the first time a trafficker recruited me. I have had many traffickers since. They all played different roles in my life. I can also vividly remember when I became "Sarah." My boyfriend at the time had a brother who was my drug dealer. He started calling me Sarah, and since I didn't want to face who I had become, it felt like starting with a clean slate. I was really hiding from God.

My first arrest happened when I was eighteen years old. I have been arrested over fifty times. I have seventeen felonies and fourteen misdemeanors. I am the poster child for institutionalization. Jail and prison had been of no consequence to me. In 2017 I heard about Hope Center Indy (HCI) for the first time. Although I was intrigued by the idea, I wasn't ready, so I did not make it. I am a runner. I run from everything. I came to HCI in August of 2018. God showed up undeniably that day. I sat in community corrections, planning to run once again. I think God must have must have been laughing at my plans. The security guard walked me to the Uber, where I still planned on running. But the Uber

178

driver got on the highway instead of driving through my neighborhood, where I had planned to get out. In that Uber, I surrendered to God. I decided to stop running. I did five months at HCI the first time and, unfortunately, was asked to leave due to inappropriate behavior on my part.

I was once again running from God and myself. The seed, however, had already been planted, and running the streets wasn't fun for me anymore. I went back to jail within months, and all I could think about was coming home to HCI. Jail was finally what it was meant to be: hard. During the first four months I was sober, I lost four people back-to-back to the streets. People I was around daily while running the streets. Once again, God had protected me by sitting me down. It is very likely that if He had not, I would have lost my life as well, just by being around one of those four people when they were murdered. I had found God's love through the many people who had touched my life through this program. Being away from it was like taking water from any living thing.

The Hope Center has been a blessing in my life. Pastor Nolen's faith in God has fueled not only this program but also my desire for a relationship with Christ. The many people involved in our lives on various levels, be it direct support staff, volunteers, or even just the people who pray for us, inspire us to walk in God's image. I had finally found the right kind of God. The one true love of my life. I found my worth in Him. I had to face many demons along the way, most of them internal. Many of those demons had such a stronghold on me. Even admitting they were there was a battle in itself. One of the hardest things I faced was admitting that I was not a nice person. See, I did not treat others well, but I was oblivious to that. I genuinely thought I was a nice person, but nothing could have been further from the truth. After several months of fighting with myself and everyone else, someone finally told me that I had to change my inner dialogue with myself to treat others well. Until I found my worth in Christ, I couldn't treat myself with respect—let alone others. I continue to grow in my faith daily and become a better person in general. I am forever grateful to the people Christ uses to edify me. If they were not walking in His will, then I might still be lost. I no longer answer to "Sarah"; I am a new creature in Christ.

Proverbs 27:17 states: "As iron sharpens iron, so one person sharpens another." I continue to learn to listen when He speaks to me. I started working with Redefined Hope Boutique toward the end of quarantine (as the boutique opened again after the Covid shutdown). I was elated to be one of the few people to actually be able to work. I had never worked retail before and hadn't worked at anything other than a desk job in twenty-two years. I was quite intimidated, really. I wondered if I would live up to others' expectations. I could not have been any more wrong. I absolutely love what I do and the people I work with. I have since gotten my certification to be a community health worker, and it is my true desire to one day be on staff with the Hope Center, so I can share God's love as it has been shared with me. I want to educate society on the lifestyle and mentality of the street to better assist with bringing people like me into His love. It is an overwhelming, never-ending, reckless kind of love that cannot be found anywhere else.

From the Mountaintop to the Valley of Despair

On tours of the Hope Center, my son David and I would often say, "The Hope Center is for everyone—for residents, staff, volunteers, and people who come to our businesses." Our mission as a ministry is to "impart hope and healing to every heart." Little did we know how true this would be for the Nolen family. The Hope Center was for us too. As you read this chapter, I pray that if you find yourself in the valley of despair, you will find the same hope we have in Christ.

Joy and Sorrow of 1991

Our son David was born Sunday morning during our worship service on January 6, 1991. He was an answer to prayer for my wife, Tonia, who wanted us to have a son after having four beautiful daughters. She had prayed and specifically asked for a son. When she got pregnant, she knew God had answered. Sure enough, David entered the world having five mothers—one mom and his four older sisters. We all so enjoyed the new member of our family. Now our family felt full.

In March of the same year, my dad died suddenly of a heart attack. This loss sent my life into mourning. At the age of thirty-six, my days were filled with waves of grief. My dad, my brother, and I had farmed together, and our relationship had grown closer over the last fifteen years.

On the day of his death, we had gone to look at another farm that was for sale. As we walked the grounds, my dad couldn't keep up. He said, "Boys, go on. I'll mosey along back to the truck." I should have seen it, but I didn't. I knew Dad had lost a lot of his strength, and his body was getting weaker, but never in my wildest dreams did I think this would be my last day on earth with him.

Three years earlier, I'd felt like I needed to have a conversation with my dad about his spiritual journey. My dad was a quiet man, never sharing his feelings with us. One evening my dad was watching TV after supper. As I went in and sat down across from him, I reached over, grabbed the remote, and turned off the TV. I said, "Dad, I have something I want to ask you and I never have. It means more to me than family and all the wonderful times we have shared together."

This got his attention.

I said, "It means more to me than anything in this world. I want to ask you, 'Have you ever accepted Jesus as your personal Savior?'"

I don't know why, but talking to your loved ones about Christ seems so difficult. I wonder why? We know they love us, but the nervous feelings we have are real.

As I paused and waited for his response, he said, "Son, I want you to know if something happens to me, I have made my peace with the Lord." For the next hour, we sat there and shared about our spiritual lives.

When I was driving home that evening, it was like a weight had been lifted off my shoulders. My heart was filled with overflowing joy. On the day of his celebration of life service, I was so glad I could share about our conversation and how Dad had received the gift of eternal life.

My dad had been the caregiver of my grandpa, "Pop" Nolen, who was ninety-one. So right after my dad's death, I decided we would take Pop into our family. My wife Tonia joined me in caring for Pop, and she was gracious enough to make the homemade gravy he requested for breakfast every morning. My grandfather had been a moonshiner in the hills of Kentucky, but at the age of fifty-six he gave his life to Christ and was beautifully changed. Pop lived with us for seven years, and during this time, he grew to love Dave. He often said that David was the smartest little boy he had ever seen. None of his sisters would have agreed with that, but it did make his parents smile. I wonder how many prayers Pop prayed over David's life during the years he lived with us.

David's Faith

David gave his life to Jesus as a young boy at the age of five. At the end of his Wednesday night Bible school class, David's teacher, who also was his mother, presented the plan of salvation to the class. On the way home from church, they stopped by the grocery store for a few items. Tonia was ready to get out of the car, but David said he wanted to ask Jesus into his heart and ask him to forgive him of his sins. Wanting to wait until they got home so his father could be a part of David's salvation experience, Tonia suggested he wait to pray with his dad as soon as they got home. David was not waiting another minute. This was an urgent matter to him. He said he wasn't waiting to go home, and he wasn't going into the store until he prayed to Jesus. So, with much joy, his mother led him in the prayer of salvation.

As David grew into his teenage years, he finally grew taller than all his sisters and even his dad. He wanted to take on the protective brother role and look after and even care for his sisters. As annoying as he sometimes was to his sisters, they never doubted his love for them. David was fun; at times he was the life of the party. I often joked that David was a walking encyclopedia of useless information. He never forgot a one-liner from a movie that was funny, and he knew just when to use it. He did some really good impersonations that would make all of us laugh. My daughters would say to me, "Dad, don't laugh at him—it will only make it worse." David loved to make me laugh, so my laughter would often cause him to keep making more jokes or doing more impersonations. David was fun, and he enjoyed life.

David grew up in the church and in a pastor's home. Even though he had accepted Jesus at the age of five, his faith truly became his own after a couple years of college. He had never strayed from his faith, but around the age of twenty-one or twenty-two, he grew exponentially in his faith. He was dating a young lady and wanted to marry her, but he was a poor college kid. So, the plan was for him to come home, get a job, save money, and do college online. All was going well until one day she told David she wanted to break off the relationship. This breakup shocked him, and he felt rejected and heartbroken. The pain of this loss turned David toward Christ. He went looking for his purpose, and he found it in Jesus.

The change in his life was noticeable. He was becoming a young man of prayer and of God's word. He would spend hours in his room studying the Bible and listening for the Spirit's prompting. His passion and love for Jesus were contagious; it was a real joy for his parents and sisters to see him becoming such a man of God. His faith was what caught my attention. He just believed God was going to do something, and he encouraged me to pray with him about it. His childlike faith was delightful to see as he prayed about his future.

One night around 2013, he came to our bedroom and knocked on the door. When he came in, he said, "Dad, God just told me to help you, whatever that is: church planting, missionary work. Whatever it is, I am supposed to help you."

Tonia and I were so happy to hear him say this. We knew this was the Holy Spirit's prompting. We had prayed that our children would want to serve Christ, so this was music to our ears. It felt like such an added blessing that David and I would be able to serve Christ together.

Serving Together

When Jesus sent out His disciples to do ministry, He sent them two by two. So in February of 2016, David and I stepped out by faith to create Hope Center Indy as a Christ-centered refuge for women coming out of human trafficking. The two of us would begin to dream together of a place where Jesus would be honored, and His life-changing power would be made available for ladies to start on their path toward healing.

What a blessing for any father to work alongside his son. For three-and-a-half years we brainstormed, dreamed, prayed, and cast the vision for this new ministry. To see Dave's gifts come alive and his leadership develop was wonderful to watch.

My wife Tonia remembers that one day Dave was giving a tour of the Hope Center to some elderly ladies. He shared stories of God's provision and updated them on the ministry. At the end of the tour, one of the ladies exclaimed, "You are the best tour guide I've ever had!"

David smiled and said, "Can you say that a little bit louder? My mom is standing right over there, and I'd like her to hear."

When he came to tell me that story, he wittily added that this elderly lady had said, "Yes, you are so much better than that old guy!" David laughed, meaning this as a joke about his dad. Tonia and I thought it was pretty funny!

In September of 2018, David said to me, "Dad, I am having some heart palpitations. I think I am going to have it checked out."

At times, if I have too much caffeine or sugar, my heart will surge like two beats being joined together, but it was never anything serious. So my advice for him was to stop drinking so much coffee. Yet he went to the doctor, and to all of our surprise, the doctor said he was born with a heart defect. He was born with a bicuspid valve for his aorta instead of a tricuspid valve. After a full examination, the doctor said, "You are young, strong, and healthy, so let's just keep an eye on it."

There was no real concern on our part. Dave had participated in sports during high school, and nothing had ever shown up during his physicals.

David met the love of his life, Stephanie, in 2018. Stephanie was a beautiful young lady who had a heart to serve Jesus, and she even laughed at all of David's jokes. It was obvious to our whole family how happy they were together. We knew David had met a winner, so all his sisters, nieces, and nephews told him to not mess this up. We are proud to say he didn't, and they were married on November 4, 2018, at the wedding barn on the campus of the Hope Center. David wanted the Hope Center residents to come to the wedding. So many of them said they had never been to a wedding before, and they thought everything was so beautiful. Maybe David and Stephanie's wedding helped these ladies believe again that they were deserving of a beautiful wedding and a loving marriage.

Because the Hope Center still had open floors that were not being used by the residential programs, David and

Stephanie moved into a staff apartment on campus. They continued to serve the Lord together at the Hope Center.

Tragedy

In January 2019, David said to me, "I am not feeling well. I think I will go back to the doctor."

This time the doctor told him the valve was not closing properly, and he would need to have his valve replaced. We did our homework and talked to the surgeon on a couple of occasions leading up to his surgery. The success rate for someone of David's age was over 95%, so we felt confident of his full recovery. As a pastor, I had attended a lot of surgeries with my church members for over forty-six years. Many of these were open-heart surgeries, and they all came through well, so I knew he would be fine.

David's surgery was on May 17, 2019, at the Indiana Heart Hospital in Indianapolis. That morning we all felt a little anxious, but our faith was strong, and we knew our Lord would see him through. After prayer, the nurses were ready to wheel him off to surgery. His wife Stephanie and his mom gave him kisses, and I assured him we would be there when he came out of surgery.

Even though David was a strong man, he had a tender heart, and he began to cry. Maybe he was feeling something in his spirit and sensed something we didn't. His surgery was eight hours long, from prep to recovery, so we kept up with his progress over a TV monitor that told us the phases he was going through. Once the operation was over, the surgeon met with all of us and said the procedure had gone perfectly. It couldn't have been better. We were all so relieved. We knew the recovery process would be slow, but we were hopeful that he would be back to full health soon.

Once home at their apartment at the Hope Center, David was progressing, and everything seemed normal. When he was fourteen days post-op, he walked down to his office and spent some time working on some things—probably reading his emails or listening to his messages. When he went back to his apartment that evening, he had some pain in his neck and a little in his chest and arm. He called the doctor's office, and they said it was pretty normal to have pain like that from this surgery. They advised him to take some pain medicine, so he did, and the pain went away.

It was around 2:30 a.m. that my wife's phone rang. I had turned my phone off and was charging it. When Tonia answered the call, it was Stephanie. She said, "Something has happened to David. Come quickly! He is not breathing."

She had called 911, and first responders were arriving. We dressed and headed to the Center as fast as we could. Not more than fifteen minutes had passed, and we were still ten to fifteen minutes from the Center when my phone rang. We were informed that they had pronounced David dead. He had passed; there was nothing they could do.

When I heard those words, they were like the sting of death, stinging my heart and soul. All I could do was cry out, "Oh, God, Oh, God." My wife was in complete shock, like her system had shut down to help her function. When we arrived at the Center, the ambulance was parked by the door. We were met by the first responders, and they said, "We moved David to the floor in the hallway outside his apartment."

We quickly climbed the three flights of stairs to see Stephanie sitting on the floor by his body. When we sat down by David and looked at his lifeless body, waves of sorrow and grief washed over us. Waves of disbelief. *It just can't be. God, NO! NO! Please, God, let him breathe. Let him live!*

Overcoming Despair

The rest of that day, we were in total shock, like we were in a fog. Friends and family came to our home to pray and cry with us. Our daughter Shari flew in from Missouri that evening, and our family relived our loss together. It just couldn't be true, but it was true—David was gone from this earth.

I can't remember if any of us slept much that night. But in the morning, I was startled as the word *despair* rang through my heart and mind. Before this moment, I don't know if I could have defined *despair,* but now I sure knew what it felt like. I was sitting on the edge of the bed crying, thinking, *I can't do this, I can't get through this*. I was despairing of life itself.

Then it was like the Holy Spirit reminded me of Paul's words in 2 Corinthians 1:8: "We do not want you to be uninformed, brothers and sisters, about the troubles we experienced in the province of Asia. We were under great pressure, far beyond our ability to endure, so that we despaired of life itself."

Only Paul knows what he meant by the phrase, "despaired of life itself." But for me, it was, *Why go on living? Why bear this pain, this loss? Death would be a welcome visitor, anything but living.* We often question why a loving God would allow us to despair of life itself. Why would the Life Giver cause us to despair of the gift of life He has given us? Paul answered my question in verse 9, "We had the sentence of death in ourselves so that we would not trust in ourselves but in God who raises the dead."

As I read this passage of Scripture, I was despairing of life itself. Then, all of a sudden, it was like the sting of death was lifted off my heart and life. I knew the God of all comfort had just reached down with His comfort and touched my life. I felt strengthened. I knew Dave was alive in heaven, enjoying his new life and his new home that had been prepared for him. From this point on, I never had this despairing feeling again. My grandpa would always say, "Look up because when you do, something good always happens." So I began to look up, for my help comes from the Lord. I can't really describe it, but the weight of despair was lifted, and I felt like I could now go on living. This does not mean I didn't feel the loss or cry about David's homegoing. I miss him, and I loved being with him, so I still have those empty feelings. When I feel this way, I just thank our Lord that David ran his race well and finished well. We rejoice in the life he lived.

For months it was like we were living in a bad dream, never to wake up. We were in shock, in a mental fog, like it couldn't be true, but it was. As a family, we did a course called "Grief Share," which was so helpful for all of us. It helped us to realize that we all grieve differently, and some days all we can do is the next thing. We realized we just had to do one thing at a time: Get out of bed, take a shower, put one foot in front of the other. We didn't try to do too much, just the next thing and then the next thing. This began to help us on our journey toward healing.

I remember dreading going back to the office the first time after David's homegoing. I knew it would hurt too much to see David's office and his desk, knowing that I wouldn't ever see him in there again. David had a couple of T-shirts he liked to wear; he had even modeled them for the Boutique. One said, "Giant Slayer," and the other said, "Faith Moves Mountains, Bro." David felt like he was a giant slayer because he had the same name as King David, who had slain Goliath. He also was a young man of faith, and he would often say, "Dad, don't pray for an open door. Ask God to put a door where there is no door!" He believed God would move mountains.

As I was driving into the office for the first time after his death, I prayed, *Lord, I need to slay some giants today and move some mountains. I need to walk by David's office to get to mine.* I mustered up enough faith and courage to walk by his office to mine. Today the wall between our offices is a memorial wall that displays three pictures of David. One is of the first time he spoke to cast the vision to create the Hope Center, and the other two pictures—you guessed it—are of him wearing his Giant Slayer and Mountain Mover T-shirts.

We had an artist take David's prayer journal and copy his handwriting. She wrote one of David's favorite quotes on the wall: "God just loves showing off by answering prayer at the Hope Center." Today the wall is a nice tribute to our co-founder.

As I walked in that morning, I made it by his office and opened my door. Someone had slipped an envelope under it. So I picked it up, walked over, and sat at my desk. I opened the envelope and inside it was a check for $50,000. As my tears flowed, I could hear David say, "Dad, God loves showing off by answering prayer at the Hope Center. Stay the course."

This moment strengthened me and helped me to keep doing the next thing.

Make Heaven Crowded

My wife Tonia has shared her moment of comfort this way at a later time: She said that when we were sitting on the floor by David's body, and she was looking into his lifeless face, she had never been so thankful for Jesus' words, "I am the resurrection and the life. He who believes in me will live even though they die. Whoever lives by believing in me will never die." Jesus, her Living Hope, gave her this promise. Without this wonderful truth, she would have despaired of life and remained in the valley of despair.

In the weeks and months to come, Tonia's grief would affect so much of her health and daily life. Tonia has always been an incredible cook and very organized in her meal preparations, but for months after Dave's passing, she found it hard to think straight to plan or prepare anything. Sometimes she would walk into a grocery store and just stare into space. Thankfully, our church family and many friends from our town brought meals for Tonia and me, our children, and grandchildren for three months after David's passing. People understood that it was hard for us to handle even the most common tasks while we were grieving. These meals gave us time to sit together with our family members almost every evening, and to continue talking about Dave, cry together, and process our grief.

One Sunday morning Tonia and I were going to church. Usually, we pray together on our way to church. As we were praying, Tonia saw a vision of Jesus to her right, but He quickly faded, and all she saw were His eyes. She continued to pray, looking at His eyes. He was looking at her with attentive eyes. As she was having her devotions on the following Tuesday morning, she turned to Psalm 34:15, "The eyes of the LORD are on the righteous, and His ears are open to their cry." She sensed that Jesus was saying to her, "I see every tear you cry, and I hear every plea for help for your broken heart."

Tonia leaned into worship and God's word and found relief for her soul. For a year and a half, almost every Sunday night, Tonia and I would head to the Prayer Center on the Hope Center campus. As just the two of us, we worshiped together, prayed together, cried together, and we found strength to face another week without David. Instead of blaming God, we blessed His name for our great hope. Instead of running from God, we ran into His loving arms. Instead of getting down on our circumstances, we got down on our knees and poured out our hearts honestly to our Heavenly Father. These simple steps served us well on our path toward healing.

That summer we had three wonderful celebrations that bought great joy to our lives as a family. We held three baptismal services. First, we met with Tonia's side of the family, and seventeen of her family members made a public confession of their faith in Jesus for the forgiveness of their sins. Then we gathered with my side of the family, and sixteen members made their confession. Then we gathered with some friends from Morristown, where my kids, including David, attended school, and twelve people who heard about these baptisms asked to be baptized as well. That summer over fifty people placed their faith in Christ for salvation.

Tonia and I had prayed for forty-three years that all our family would experience the joy and hope we had found in Christ. Now they all had. We saw forty-three years of prayers answered that summer. We know God didn't need to use David's death to bring our family to Him, but He never fails to use our loss and pain to bring something wonderful out of it. I know David would say, "Whatever way God uses to get them to heaven is great. Just get everyone here!"

My granddaughter Raegan wears a T-shirt that says, "Make Heaven Crowded." That is exactly what we are trying to do.

Tonia and I can hardly wait to get to heaven and have the best tour guide the Hope Center has ever had show us around our heavenly home.

Promises to Read

John 11:25: "Jesus said to her, 'I am the resurrection and the life. The one who believes in me will live, even though they die.'"

2 Corinthians 1:3–8: "Blessed be the God and Father of our Lord Jesus Christ, the Father of mercies and God of all comfort, who comforts us in all our affliction so that we will be able to comfort those who are in any affliction with the comfort with which we ourselves are comforted by God. For just as the sufferings of Christ are ours in abundance, so also our comfort is abundant through Christ. But if we are afflicted, it is for your comfort and salvation; or if we are comforted, it is for your comfort, which is effective in the patient enduring of the same sufferings which we also suffer; and our hope for you is firmly grounded, knowing that as you are partners in our sufferings, so also you are in our comfort. For we do not want you to be unaware, brothers and sisters, of our affliction which occurred in Asia, that we were burdened excessively, beyond our strength, so that we despaired even of life."

Psalm 34:15: "The eyes of the LORD are on the righteous, and His ears are open to their cry."

Psalm 121:1-2: "I lift up my eyes to the mountains-- where does my help come from? My help comes from the LORD, the Maker of heaven and earth."

Prayer to Pray

Lord, I know You are close to the brokenhearted, and You save those who are crushed in spirit. I ask You to help all who are feeling the brokenness that comes from loss in our lives. Please put our hearts and lives back together. Let us know Your hope and comfort. I ask this in Jesus' name, Amen.

David Nolen speaking about Hope Center Indy

Pastor Hubert and David Nolen

Memorial wall for David Nolen in the staff hallway at Hope Center Indy

11

Upside Down

Sometimes we say that David, our associate director, has been promoted to heaven. We know that David is alive in heaven, enjoying his new life and his new home, which has been prepared for him. But we are still here, with our feet on the earth, and we have to go on without him.

I didn't realize the ripple effect his death would have on the whole organization—our governing board, our staff, and our residents. David's death cascaded through our ministry like a heavy weight placed on all our hearts, turning our world upside down. In the last chapter, I mentioned my first day back on campus without David and how I had to pray that the Lord would help me slay the giants of grief and mourning and move the mountain of sorrow from my life. I quickly realized I wasn't the only one working through the mourning process.

Board

In 2016 and 2017, David and I had many conversations and meetings as we selected each of our founding board members. When our dreams were big but our budget was small, our board gathered faithfully once a month around the conference table in David's office to put the foundation of the organization together. Over the first few years of serving together as a board, David often said to me, "Dad, I love our board. They are such high-quality individuals with great hearts." He cherished their support and all they did to help us create and govern this ministry.

The board members enjoyed David's enthusiasm to see the Hope Center grow. They were able to be part of his leadership growth and his personal growth in those years. They were able to see David's big smile when he told them the news that he had proposed to Stephanie at a beach on Lake Michigan. They congratulated him when they saw his wedding photos, him standing next to his bride. Then, when David told them the news of his heart condition and how he would need open heart surgery, they circled around him as he sat in his chair and prayed for him. The board members were just as shocked and heartbroken as everyone else when they received the phone call on May 31, 2019, that David had died.

I remember our first board meeting after David had passed. Our board gathered where we always did—around the conference table in David's office. As we started, the board shared how hard it was for all of them to walk on campus, knowing they were headed to David's office but that David wouldn't be sitting at the table with us. As we talked that day, they voiced their love for David and what his life had meant to them. They all had seen firsthand his impact on creating the Hope Center.

Staff

One of the first responsibilities that David had as associate director was to put together our residential program staff. As he read over resumes and prayed for direction, he began to put together a team that he felt confident would guide our residents well on their pathway to healing. Some of our staff were closer to David as the associate director than they were to me. David was the one who met with them during the hiring process and continued to connect with them on a weekly basis. By 2019, the Hope Center had at least fifteen staff members, and many of these staff members had a close working relationship with David and enjoyed serving with him.

On the day David died, many of our Hope Center staff members gathered in the Prayer Center to pray together for our family and for each other as they tried to make sense of this sudden tragedy. The following week, they all came to David's viewing and Celebration of Life service to support our family, cry with us, honor David's impact on them, and thank God for his life. We were so grateful for those who stepped into our circle of pain, helped lift the weight off our hearts, and shared our loss.

Our staff had to grieve what losing David meant for each of them. He was their sounding board and ongoing support. For some of them, they felt they had lost the one who believed in them. His coworkers missed seeing his face during their daily routines—stepping into his office to get advice or encouragement, eating lunch next to him in the cafeteria, hearing his laughter in the hallways, and hearing his prayers in the Prayer Center. There was no denying it: His faith and his personality were big. Suddenly, his presence was missing at the Center. The void of his leadership and friendship was felt by all. It would take some time to get a bounce back in our step and unshackle ourselves from the heavy grief we all carried.

Residents

The residents at the Hope Center had gotten to know David when they saw him every Wednesday evening in the Prayer Center for our weekly prayer meeting. Sometimes David filled in to teach one of the classes for the residents if any of their teachers needed a substitute for the day. The residents liked David's sense of humor and his God stories, which were descriptions of answers to prayer that he had experienced.

A few weeks after David's passing, I remember going back to the Hope Center to teach my class on basic principles of living a Christian life. On that day, I was surprised to hear the residents talk freely about how they feared they would need to look for a new program and another place to live. They thought for sure I would be closing the Hope Center. They had seen me with my son often and knew how much I loved him. They thought losing David would break me and render my faith useless. They were worried that the Hope Center would now be completely out of hope!

Most of them were used to people quitting and walking away when things were overwhelming. But when they saw my family and me not walking away but keep walking toward Christ, it was our greatest witness. Our residents saw my daughter Rachel still working as a director in our boutique, my daughter Sara working shifts for our residential staff, my daughter-in-law Stephanie still living in the apartment on campus that she had shared with David, and my wife still mentoring some of the residents, volunteering sometimes in the Boutique and the food pantry, and coming to Wednesday prayer meetings and important Hope Center events with me. Our residents saw the vulnerable look of grief and sometimes fresh tears on our faces in those first months after David's death, but the residents also saw us praying and worshiping God, even in our pain. When we pressed into Christ and ran to His comfort and care, it helped them know Christ was real. We all suffer great losses, but how we handle them lets all who are watching see if our faith is real.

One of the things that helped us as a family was that we let people know we loved to talk about David or hear how David had touched their lives. We shared that talking about David brought us joy, not pain. We enjoyed laughing about his sayings or the pranks he would play on his friends. There was something about these special memories that brought comfort to our hearts. My daughter Rachel remembers that one day, while she was in the Boutique, she and a few others were talking about David not long after he had passed. They began talking about heaven and looking forward to being reunited with David in heaven. One of our residents who was an employee in the Boutique was with them during this conversation. Afterward, she told Rachel, "I think it's cool how you guys talk about seeing David again in heaven like you really mean it." Rachel smiled and told her that's why we have hope—that even though David died on earth, because of his salvation in Jesus, he's alive in heaven!

Mary Joining Our Team

After a couple of months, our residents knew that not only were we not closing the Center, but we now had an even greater purpose and passion to carry on this good work. David's departure left a big hole in our organization that I needed to fill. I needed to begin looking for a new associate director. My role as executive director is that I am a visionary person, and I am focused on the big relationships the Hope Center has with our donors and partners. After having been a pastor for over forty years, I knew my leadership style well enough to know that I needed an associate director to help run the staff and be more detail-oriented to implement the vision and coordinate teams. I knew it was important for our organization to have both the executive director and associate director in place.

Just a few weeks after David's death, a few people started to mention to me that they felt God was going to lead my daughter Mary to this position. At the time, Mary was leading the children's ministry and women's ministry at Brookville Road Community Church, where I had pastored. Mary had been there for ten years and loved her ministry. In fact, Mary had worked on staff with me there for seven years before I stepped out to start the Hope Center. Mary had felt called to ministry when she was in college and had later gone on to graduate from seminary while she was working at the church. She loved teaching the Bible, shepherding the children at the church, and leading teams of volunteers to work together.

A few people began asking Mary if she would consider going to work at the Hope Center. I hadn't talked to her about it yet because I knew she was struggling with her brother's death. She and Dave had been only three years apart in age, and his death was a shock to her world. She was honest that she was grieving so much that she couldn't think straight, and she didn't have the capacity to make a big life decision yet. When I did ask her to pray about coming, I didn't want her to feel any pressure from me. I wanted her to discern God's leading for her life and decide for herself if this might be the next chapter.

In addition to Mary's calling to ministry, her training at seminary, and her leadership experience at the church, I knew Mary had learned firsthand about imparting hope and healing—which is the mission of the Hope Center. In January 2016, Mary became licensed as a foster mom and adopted two middle school sisters, Anna and Gabby. Day by day, she walked with her daughters to overcome the challenges they were facing. She learned everything she could about trauma, abandonment, abuse, generational cycles, and most importantly, that healing is possible. Mary persevered, and Gabby and Anna persevered, and God was faithful to comfort them through the pain along the way. I know this for sure: as Mary helped her daughters through life's challenges, our Lord was preparing her to come to the Hope Center. Mary found out what it takes to walk with someone and to not give up but to see them through to a better place. Today we are so grateful Gabby and Anna are not only part of Mary's family, but also part of ours as well. We are so proud of them.

After a few months of praying about the decision to leave the job she loved at her church, Mary did finally say yes. She joined our team at the Hope Center in October of 2019, just four months after David's death.

E.O.S

We were so thankful to have Mary join our Hope Center team, but my family and I and many of our staff were still grieving. In a way, we were still walking around in a fog. It took all our mental, emotional, and physical energy to keep the ministry running. We were praying for wisdom and asking God to give us what we needed to keep moving the ministry forward. In our season of grieving, God was gracious to provide the Hope Center with a businessman named Dale Cooper and his daughter Samantha to introduce us to something called Entrepreneurial Operating System (E.O.S.).

Dale met with us to explain the E.O.S. process, and our Hope Center leaders saw this as a way to help us become more organized, more efficient, and raise the bar in every area of our ministry. We knew the process was going to be a lot of work, but we welcomed the guidance and the order. We felt like it was an answer to prayer. In January 2020, Dale and Samantha began volunteering their time to meet with our Hope Center executive team for a whole day every quarter to walk through the E.O.S. principles and to help us implement the E.O.S. process in our organization. E.O.S. is an incredibly helpful tool, but our staff has had to put in the effort to make it work. I am proud to say that our staff has worked so hard, and that is why we are seeing results.

Mary is now the integrator for the Executive Team (which is part of the E.O.S. process) to help us stay on track to accomplish our goals and to solve daily issues that may arise. Mary has done an amazing job of putting together our "A Team" for our residential ministry. Her leadership has helped move the Center forward at a reasonable pace. What has been accomplished is nothing short of remarkable since she joined our team.

As I look back, I am so thankful that God provided E.O.S. to guide us and help lead our organization, especially when we were still in such a vulnerable place emotionally. God was faithful to be our good Shepherd and to "guide us along the right paths for his name's sake" as He promises to do in Psalm 23:3.

Upside-Down Things

One of the gifts I cherish is David's prayer journal. After David passed, I found his prayer journal in his leather work bag. I read through the prayers he had prayed for our family, the Hope Center, and his personal life.

At the time of his passing, David was working on a botanical prayer garden on our campus. He dreamed of a beautiful place where the ladies could enjoy God's creation. He liked the yard outside the Prayer Center because it would be an inviting space for those who come to pray. He met with a landscape architect and had the plans drawn up. He worked with churches and businesses to provide the materials to create the garden. We had the day scheduled to start, but then there was heavy rain all day, so we had to reschedule.

When David passed, we forgot about the plans for the botanical prayer garden for months. Finally, I picked up David's architectural plans one day, and with the help of churches, businesses, and individuals, we were able to make those plans a reality. In David's prayer journal, I read that he was trying to come up with a name for the botanical garden. He had jotted down several names. Later I found this sentence, "The garden needs to be named, 'The Garden of Peace.'" So that's what we named it. We dedicated The

Garden of Peace in David's memory on the one-year anniversary of his homegoing.

One of the unique things about the garden is that we have an upside-down tree. I got this idea when my wife Tonia and I went to Alaska, and we saw an upside-down tree in a botanical garden. Tonia's siblings and their spouses had all planned this special trip to Alaska for a long time. David passed away about five weeks before we were supposed to leave on this trip. It was especially hard for Tonia to leave home so soon after David's death, but we decided to still go on this trip and be with family. Seeing the beauty of the mountains and the ocean encouraged our hearts. On the day we visited the botanical garden, the upside-down tree stood out to me.

When we returned to campus, I thought it would be beautiful to craft an upside tree in our botanical garden. We cut down a tree, leaving a trunk about twelve feet high. Then we dug up the roots. We buried the trunk in the ground, which left the roots about eight feet in the air. Each year we plant beautiful flowers in the root system of the tree, and during the summer, they grow down over the roots, making a beautiful arrangement of flowers. It really is something amazing to see; we hope to add more upside-down trees in the future.

When I think about the upside-down tree, it reminds me of life. At times, losses can turn our lives and our world upside down. Our lives get inverted, like a car rolling over and landing on its top with the four wheels pointing upward. When life has rolled us over, we can become disoriented and capsized, not knowing what to do.

What if in those moments, we take the circumstances of our lives and make a masterpiece, a work of art—something beautiful out of all the brokenness. When we see the flowers blooming and growing in our upside-down tree, it is a reminder to everyone on our campus. With eyes of hope, we can see our lives becoming something beautiful. Even when we don't know how we will move forward, God will provide us with what we need to keep living for Him, even when our lives are upside down.

Promises to Read

Psalm 23:1,3: "The LORD is my shepherd, I lack nothing. He makes lie down in green pastures... He guides me along the right paths for his name's sake."

Psalm 147:3: "He heals the brokenhearted and binds up their wounds."

Isaiah 61:1: "The Spirit of the Sovereign LORD is on me, because the LORD has anointed me to proclaim good news to the poor. He has sent me to bind up the brokenhearted, to proclaim freedom to the captives and release from darkness for the prisoners."

Prayer to Pray

Lord, for all who find themselves upside down in their life, I ask you to make something beautiful out of their circumstances. Heal and bind up their hearts; help them to trust You for another tomorrow filled with Your beauty. In Jesus' name, Amen.

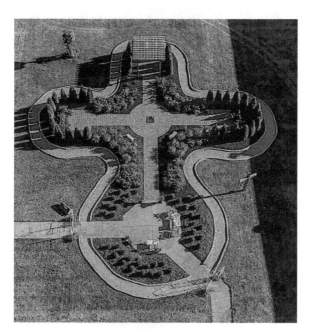

Aerial view of the botanical garden

Some of the Nolen family members after working on the upside-down tree

Upside-Down Tree in the botanical garden

12

Arrows of Discouragement

In the midst of the miraculous provision and exciting progress God has granted the Hope Center, we have faced some serious trials and discouragement, as well. Early in 2017, David and I met with Dr. Jeff Barrows, the founder of Gracehaven, a facility in Ohio for minors who are survivors of trafficking. Dr. Barrows taught some training courses for our staff and volunteers. He also told David and me that we needed to realize that providing residential care for survivors of sex trafficking meant that there was a high likelihood that our Center would be accused of sexual abuse at some point. He said to us, "It's not *if* you get accused; it's *when*." Little did we know that his words would be true.

But first, I would like to share about some of the arrows of discouragement I have faced throughout my ministry. My hope is to encourage you to keep trusting God and persevering in faith, even when you find yourself hit by the sting of arrows.

In my high school physical education class, we practiced archery. We would set up our round targets, gather our bow and arrows, step back the allowed number of steps, and practice shooting our arrows at the target. Because all of us were beginners, none of us were any good at actually hitting the target. Most of the time, the arrows would fall short or fly to either side but seldom hit the target. When it was my turn to shoot, I steadied my bow, drew the arrow, and just as I let go of the arrow, I saw a classmate walking behind the target to pick up his arrow. When I saw him, my heart sank. I wanted to yell, "Fore!" but that was the wrong sport. My arrow sailed over the top of the target, and just as the classmate turned his back to pick up his arrow, my arrow hit him square in the back. No kidding. A perfect hit—just the wrong target. Thankfully, the arrow dropped powerlessly to the ground and didn't leave a mark on my classmate's back.

Our enemy Satan draws his bow and fires his arrows in our direction, hoping to inflict pain on our lives. He targets our hearts. His flaming arrows are fear, doubt, unbelief, discouragement, angry words, bitterness, and false accusations. His arrows are many, and they keep flying our direction. The apostle Paul says in Ephesians 6:16 that we are to "take up our shield of faith, with which we can extinguish all the flaming arrows of the evil one." We need to take up our shield of faith because when the day of evil comes—and it will come—we will be able to stand our ground.

During my pastoral ministry at my church, I preached a message on Job 4:3–4: "Think how you have instructed many, how you have strengthened feeble hands. Your words have supported those who stumbled; you have strengthened faltering knees." (I mentioned this verse previously in Chapter 2, "From the Pig Pen to the Pulpit." I hope you can see that it has made an impact on my life.) Like Job, I always wanted my words to strengthen people who were collapsing under the burdens of life! I wanted my words to lift them up and set them on their feet again.

Another challenge for me was found in 1 Samuel 3:19. It was also said of the prophet Samuel that the Lord was with Samuel as he grew up, and he let none of Samuel's words fall to the ground! To my understanding, this verse says that God can take our words and use them for His purpose, even for His glory. Or He can allow our words to fall to the ground and accomplish nothing.

I am sad to say that many words I have spoken have fallen to the ground and have not accomplished any eternal glory for our Lord! My words, instead of accomplishing anything of value or purpose, were destructive in nature. For those words, I sincerely repent and ask for forgiveness. I trust God will erase them from people's memories and allow my callous, reckless, hurtful words to fall to the ground and become nothing. Or even those spoken against me.

Arrows of Words

Shortly after taking over the Hope Center campus, my son David and I were asked if we would come to a meeting with a local anti-trafficking organization. We agreed and were looking forward to partnering together against trafficking! David was not feeling well that morning, so I said, "Why don't you just wait in the car?"

So, David sat in the car while I went into the meeting.

When I went in, there were warm greetings, and we went to a conference area with a table and chairs. After introductions, the chairperson began to question me. Quickly, I realized I had been invited there to be interrogated. They wanted to know why two men were starting a ministry for trafficked women. They asked me, "Are you and your son trying to start your own brothel?"

This question shocked me. I had been a pastor at the same church in a nearby community for thirty-three years. My character and my sincere compassion to help others had shown itself to be true by the longevity of my service to my church and my community. If this group had only called some of the church staff, board of elders, or other leaders in the community who had known me for decades to inquire about my character, they would have realized that I would never do the thing they had just asked me about.

The chairperson and others in this meeting were clearly angry that Dave and I were starting this ministry when they believed we did not know what we were doing when it came to helping women who had been trafficked. For over an hour, I tried to answer their cutting questions.

I tried to share the vision with them that the Hope Center would be a place that would allow for multiple layers of leadership and staff without David or I playing the role of the program director or a case manager. This group was so focused on the fact that I didn't have experience interacting with women who had been trafficked that they missed the important fact that I could hire women leaders who did, and I could partner with people who could offer the resources our residents would require. David and I didn't intend to work with the women on a daily basis—our program staff would do that. I wanted to emphatically tell them that our goal was absolutely not to hurt or traumatize anyone, but they would not hear it. Our goal was to help women have a safe place to heal and provide the resources and services to equip them to get back on their feet. David and I were focused on fundraising for the cost of the facility and program needs, cultivating partnerships, and providing spiritual direction for the organization as a whole. But in the minds of the people sitting in that conference room, they could not see how this arrangement could work, and they distrusted all our intentions.

After leaving the meeting, I felt grateful David had been sick that morning and did not participate. If he hadn't been sick beforehand, he definitely would have been sick after the meeting.

After the meeting that day, I wrote these words in my prayer journal: *Lord, today's meeting was disheartening. I feel discouraged. But why? I felt unprepared for some of their questions and looked down upon. Yet, I wanted to work together. Help me to check my heart, my pride, and surrender all ill feelings to You and Your Spirit. I know that Hope Center Indy will never be created, Lord, unless You do it. Unless God does it, it will never happen!"*

I worked through the emotions of hearing those words of discouragement and continued to connect with other partners who had experience and expertise in this ministry work. Despite those harsh words, we persevered and saw the ministry grow.

Arrow of False Accusation

Unfortunately, there was another arrow coming that I hadn't foreseen. On Tuesday, May 12, 2020, at 10:00 a.m., our staff headed to the Prayer Center for weekly worship and prayer. It was a beautiful day, and a good friend was leading worship for us. We had just started the service when I discovered the campus fire alarm had gone off. We have safety protocols in place, so I knew everyone would be following the procedure. The Prayer Center is in a separate building, so we weren't affected by the fire alarm and continued our worship.

Then a staff member came up to me and said, "All kinds of police officers are on campus!"

I said, "I know. Todd Jordan and the K9 division for electronic detection is here with six officers and their dogs. They are using our campus for training because they will be going on a search warrant tomorrow."

As we continued to worship, another staff member came up to me and said, "The police are asking for you."

So, I headed out of the Prayer Center and was met by two police officers. They said they wanted to ask me a few questions. "Would you be willing to go downtown to IMPD (Indianapolis Metropolitan Police Department) and cooperate with the investigation?"

I was led to the captain who, I then found out, was actually leading a search of our campus. After a brief introduction with some very vague words and very little information on why they were on our campus, I finally realized that they were there to investigate accusations against the Hope Center. I asked if I needed an attorney.

The captain replied, "It's up to you. You can if you want to, but you don't have to."

I paused, taking this situation in. I said, "I will be in my office."

I called my daughter Sara, who is an attorney. Sara called Attorney Mike Boring, whose office is near the Hope Center. Mike arrived on our campus within twenty minutes.

Let me say first and foremost that I support our local police and am thankful how they work hard to protect our community. If I'm ever in need of help, the police would be the first I'd call! We understand that the police were there to do their job to investigate the allegations.

When the investigations began, we were completely caught off guard, and no one knew what the police were referring to. During that moment, everything became like a fog. I was thinking, "What is going on?"

By asking the officers questions, our attorney discovered that two former residents had made accusations of sexual abuse against a volunteer and another person we did not know. This shocked all of us. None of the alleged incidents had ever been reported to any staff, volunteer, other resident, or any other individual within Hope Center Indy, during the time these residents had participated in our program. Our current residents at the time were questioned on this day about their safety, and all the residents gave a positive account of their experiences at Hope Center Indy.

We cooperated fully. Investigators searched every hallway and every room of our facilities. Nothing was retrieved during the search that would have validated any criminal conduct. When they finished the search, the captain said he would contact our lawyer in a day or so for an interview with me. My attorney informed him that we would make ourselves available at their request.

While we waited for Indianapolis Metropolitan Police Department (IMPD) to call, we commissioned our attorney to conduct an internal investigation to make sure we did our due diligence in following up with this matter. He conducted staff interviews, reviewed our policies and procedures, and checked our security protocols. His internal investigation identified several indisputable factors concluding that the allegations could not have occurred as described.

We understand that the police needed to do their job and follow up on any allegations. But there is also the other side of the story of how people are affected when false allegations are made, and police take over people's apartments and workplaces with a warrant. For about five hours that day, the staff and residents on our campus were traumatized by this search. I was in my office for the duration of the search, but other staff members told me how the residents were reacting outside. The police had surrounded the group of residents as they had made them sit outside on the grass, separated from some of the staff members. Several residents started trembling because seeing so many police officers brought back bad memories. One resident told us later, "My whole life, I hadn't felt safe. Then, after being here for seven months, I had forgotten what it felt like to *not* feel safe. But today was the first day in seven months that I didn't feel safe here."

Another resident told staff, "I was so angry at them for coming in and saying these things about the place that saved my life."

Another resident had an interesting story to tell us about that day. She explained to us that she used to know a policer officer who had often been there during her previous arrests for drug charges. He had been compassionate toward her and had often given her snacks as she was on her way to jail. She explained that she usually wouldn't eat for about three days in jail because the food was so disgusting. This was why she had asked the officer to start bringing her snacks. She saw this officer again on this day because he was one of the officers on campus with the search warrant. She walked up to him and said hi. He was surprised to see her and said, "I haven't seen you in over a year! I thought you were dead.

Any time an unidentified body was found, I would go check to make sure it wasn't you."

She said, "I've been here for over a year, and I'm thirteen months sober!"

He smiled and said, "If this place can help you, then this place can help anybody."

This was a story that made us smile amid this stressful time. We waited for the promised phone call from the captain, but it never came. We requested the affidavits from the ladies' accusations, and it took about a month to get them. Month after month, our attorney reached out to the captain and lead investigator on the case, but they never responded to his emails or phone calls. We offered numerous opportunities for official interviews with anyone IMPD desired to speak to. None of Hope Center's staff members, including myself, were ever officially interviewed by IMPD about this investigation. We were simply left to wait for months.

The Arrow Pointed at Me

In the affidavits, I saw that I was being accused of sexual abuse by one of our former residents. To say I was stunned would have been an understatement. I was shocked and confused by the things I was being accused of.

A lot goes through your mind the first few days. *What will people think? I have pastored for forty-six years . . . and now this.* Wherever I went, I felt like all eyes were upon me.

It was hard to take James' advice in James 1:2 to count it all joy when you face trials of many kinds. I wanted to push back, but what was the best response? I felt the Lord had given me several promises from His word. The first promise was Isaiah 54:17: "No weapon formed against you will prosper; And every tongue that accuses you in judgment you will condemn. This is the heritage of the servants of the LORD, and their vindication is from Me," declares the LORD. Another verse the Lord gave me during that time was Psalm 37:6: "He will bring forth your righteousness as the light and your judgment as the noonday."

During the months while we waited on news from the investigation, my wife Tonia and I took a weeklong vacation at The Cove, the Billy Graham Association Retreat Center in North Carolina. Dr. R. T. Kendall was teaching on the Sermon on the Mount from Matthew 5–7. When he was teaching on the beatitudes in chapter 5, he said the Greek phrase that is translated in English as "Blessed are you" could also be translated as "Congratulations to you." He talked about how the beatitudes were like a ladder, each rung taking us higher into discipleship; each step graduating us into new levels of commitment.

Dr. Kendall came to the last beatitude in Matthew 5:11 and 12, "Blessed are you when people insult you, persecute you and falsely say all kinds of evil against you because of Me, rejoice and be glad because great is your reward in heaven; for in the same way they persecuted the prophets who were before you." With this beatitude, Dr. Kendall said, "Congratulations to you when people insult you, persecute you, and say all kinds of evil against you!" He jokingly said, "When you reach this level of discipleship, you were called up from the minor league to the major league."

I have always wanted to be Christlike, yet I haven't always liked the transforming process. Going from the minor league to the major league was difficult and really painful. I wanted to count it all joy. I wanted to say, "Blessed are you," and "Congratulations." But to be honest, it took the wind out of my sails. Yet the whole time I never took my eyes off Christ, and we kept praying the truth would prevail. After our class with Dr. Kendall, Tonia and I would often look at each other, smile, and say, "Congratulations."

The Arrow of Written Media

Over the next several months, we reached out to the police about a dozen times, offering to meet and request they come to do their investigation. We wanted to be exonerated. Six months passed, and still there was no response from the police. *The Indianapolis Star* was tipped off that the Center was under investigation for sexual abuse and that I, the director, was one of the accused. A reporter called and left me a message that he wanted to talk with me. I returned his call and invited him to come out, do his own investigation, and see our ministry at the Center. I told him I would answer any questions he had. He could talk to our staff or any volunteer who was willing to speak with him. He wanted to know if he could talk to our attorney, and I said yes.

After talking with our attorney, he said, "It doesn't sound like there's a story here, but I will talk to my editor, and I will keep you informed."

He never came to our campus and never asked anyone else at the Center any questions. Yet the reporter informed us via email that the Star would be running his article, and so they did. It was published on October 15, 2020—on the front page. The title of the article was, "IMPD Investigates Rape Allegations at Faith-Based Center for Survivors of Human Trafficking." It had a picture of our sign, our campus, and a photo of me. Never in my wildest dreams did I think my picture would be front-page news for sexual abuse.

Over the next several weeks, I was scheduled to speak at several churches during their Sunday morning services. I called the pastors of each of these churches and said, "I don't want to cause you or your church any heartache by having me speak. If you want to cancel the engagement, I completely understand."

Yet none of them did. They said, "Pastor, we know you. Please come and share about your ministry."

Polygraph

I talked to my attorney about doing a polygraph. Because the police had never interviewed me, I hadn't had a chance to share my side of the story. I felt like stepping forward to take a polygraph was one way I could try to prove my innocence. I was willing to pay for it myself. My attorney did not encourage it but said he would set it up if I would like him to. So, on October 26, 2020, I went to do a polygraph. I went to a clinical forensic polygraph examiner who is a twenty-one-year veteran of law enforcement, is certified in forensic psychophysiology, has completed advanced training in sexual abuse testing and terrorism testing techniques, and is an associate member of the American Polygraph Association (APA). I was calm because I knew I had nothing to deny or hide. Yet the thirty minutes of interrogation before the test were difficult. The examiner interrogated me with accusatory questions and challenged me on my answers. For instance:

"Do you view porn?"

"No."

"You sure you don't watch or look at porn?"

"No, I do not."

"You know you will flunk this test?"

"I don't view, watch, or look at porn."

"Everyone says that. You think you're innocent. Everyone who sits in that chair says they're innocent."

He really did a good job of getting my blood pressure up and my nerves on edge.

When he was ready to start the test, he hooked me up to monitors to gauge my heart rate, blood pressure, and breathing. He had the affidavit of the lady's accusations against me as he asked me ten questions. He did three tests asking the same ten questions and averaged the scores of my responses to the questions from all three tests, so he could get a good reading.

When he was finished, he said, "How do you think you did?"

I said, "I passed, but to be honest the experience was harder than I had expected."

He said, "You passed. You can bring in your lawyer now."

I left the room to get him. When we came back in and sat down, he said to us, "If I were you, I would send this report to IMPD tomorrow, and it should close your case."

I know there are different polygraphs with different scoring systems. For the particular test I took, this is how you would interpret my score: A score from -.3 to .3 on the test is inconclusive—it's unclear whether the person is lying or telling the truth. A score from -.3 to -.10 indicates that the person is definitely lying. A score from .3 to .10 means that they are definitely telling the truth. My score was .9859 out of .10, which was almost a perfect score, indicating that I was being completely honest. This is why he said, "It will close your case."

Our attorney prepared a letter with a copy of the polygraph and sent it to the IMPD captain, the chief of police, and the mayor to ask them to close our case and exonerate us of all charges. But we heard nothing back. After a few more months, the reporter from *The Indianapolis Star* reached out again to our attorney, wanting to do a follow-up story. He sent some questions and wanted to talk more about where everything stood. When the reporter reached out to IMPD, to his surprise, he was told the case had been closed, and no one affiliated with the Hope Center would be charged.

When the reporter informed us that the case had been closed, this was the first time we heard anything about the case being closed. The police never contacted us after the day of the search warrant. The conclusion that anyone with a law enforcement background would draw is that nothing was found on the day of the search. It was not only that there wasn't enough evidence to charge anyone. It was that there was zero evidence that these accusations were true. Since that time, we have been informed by a police officer that they knew the accusations were false the very next day after the search warrant.

Yet the heartache caused to me, my family, and the Center is hard to measure. For forty-six years of ministry, I have tried to live above reproach, to be blameless. I never wanted to bring disgrace to the name of Christ or His church. Yet, false accusations can destroy everything you lived for in just moments. This is why one of the Ten Commandments is "You shall not bear false witness." The damage done by reckless lies can destroy the lives of people.

Turning Arrows of Discouragement into Arrows of Praise

Today we are excited to say that the allegations are behind us, and we are in the process of winning back those who once supported us but pulled back because of this untruthful accusation. We have also worked hard to build new partnerships. In March of 2021, HCI was pleased to announce a new relationship with Operation Underground Railroad. Operation Underground Railroad is a nonprofit in Utah committed to rescuing trafficking victims and arresting perpetrators. Over the last decade, "O.U.R. has made a significant impact in the fight to end sex trafficking and sexual exploitation by assisting in rescuing and supporting thousands of survivors in 30 countries and 50 U.S. states."[ix]

We were introduced to O.U.R. through Todd Jordan, founder of Jordan Detection K9. This organization trains dogs to sniff out electronic devices. When law enforcement officers go on search warrants, seeking evidence to arrest traffickers (particularly people creating and distributing child pornography), these dogs help them find the electronic devices the perpetrators have hidden in places the officers cannot find on their own. As of 2021, Jordan Detection K9 dogs have found evidence to arrest hundreds of perpetrators who have been sexually exploiting children.

Since 2017, Todd Jordan has been using spare rooms at the Hope Center to train his dogs and handlers. (These are the same electronic detection dogs that were on our campus on the day of the search warrant.) Todd was using his family's garage as a kennel while he trained them, which meant he only had a limited capacity and could only train a small number of dogs at a time. O.U.R. wanted to give him the ability to work at full capacity by helping him build a K9 barn. Todd approached me in 2019, requesting to build his K9 barn on our campus. I knew this was an incredible cause to be a part of, and so, after some planning, we decided to move forward with this option. Operation Underground Railroad donated $700,000 to build a new K9 Training Center on our campus.

On March 12, 2021, Jordan Detection K9 held their dog training graduation in our Hope Center Ballroom. We decided to hold a groundbreaking ceremony for the K9 Barn immediately following the dog graduation. Many people from Operation Underground Railroad flew in from Utah and all over the U.S. to come to the graduation and groundbreaking ceremony. On that day about thirty to forty police officers and various other national anti-trafficking leaders came to our campus to support Jordan Detection K9 and Hope Center Indy.

My daughter Mary said that when she walked into the Ballroom that day and saw all those law enforcement officers, electronic detection dogs, and national anti-trafficking leaders, she started to tear up, overwhelmed with emotion that God was bringing restoration to our relationship with law enforcement and affirming our work to national leaders. Today, in 2022, the construction of the K9 Barn is completed, and our partnerships with Jordan Detection K9 and Operation Underground Railroad have continued to grow. Together we are training electronic detection dogs on our campus to equip law enforcement to prosecute perpetrators in child exploitation cases.

I probably don't need to remind you that our spiritual journey is filled with many arrows of discouragement. At times we are all tempted to give up and quit. Yet we know that Jesus did not say it would be easy—just that He would be with us! I am so thankful that Jesus was with my family and me as we walked through these fiery trials.

I don't know what trial you may be facing or what arrow has been shot your way, but don't quit. Don't give up. Use your shield of faith to fend off the arrows of discouragement. Keep on until you see the victory or hear Matthew 5:12: "Blessed are you when people insult you, persecute you, and falsely say all kinds of evil against you because of me. Rejoice and be glad, because great is your reward in heaven." Blessed are you, and great is your reward!

Promises to Read:

Psalm 11:2: "In the Lord I take refuge . . . For look, the wicked bend their bows; they set their arrows against the strings, to shoot from the shadows at the upright in heart."

Job 4:3–6: "Think how you have instructed many, how you have strengthened feeble hands. Your words have supported those who stumbled; you have strengthened faltering knees. But now trouble comes to you, and you are discouraged; it strikes you, and you are dismayed. Should not your piety be your confidence and your blameless ways your hope?"

Genesis 50:20: "As for you, you meant evil against me, but God meant it for good."

Prayer to Pray:

Jesus, I ask for everyone who is facing arrows of discouragement or even false accusations in some way that You would strengthen them. Give each person the grace needed to respond in a Christlike manner. Help them to keep their eyes on You and allow You to be their defender. In Your precious name, Amen.

Ribbon-cutting ceremony for the opening of the K9 Barn on the Hope Center Indy campus

13

Giving Engines

In this book, I have shared a lot about the issue of money. I've shared how I've had to learn to trust God to provide for me personally and also how God has provided incredible blessings of furniture, equipment, supplies, and miraculous financial gifts to the Hope Center. I'm sure that in your life, you have also spent a lot of time, attention, and prayer discerning how to best make and budget the necessary money for your family, nonprofit, and/or business. In this chapter, I'd like to share yet another dimension I have learned while seeking God for the finances to meet the Hope Center budget.

One of the unique things about the Hope Center is our goal of having our "giving engines" cover half of our annual budget. We have used the phrase "giving engines" to describe any business that works to bring income into the Center as an ongoing fundraiser. (Often other organizations refer to these as social enterprises, but I like saying "giving engines" because an engine gives a vehicle the power to move forward at a greater speed. I like thinking of our HCI giving engines as sources of empowerment to move us forward in our long-term goals.) As of the time of this writing, these giving engines include our three boutiques, two coffee shops, a beauty salon, a wedding barn, formal ballroom, a greenhouse, and contract manufacturing. Currently, our giving engines bring in the funds to cover about 20% of our annual budget, but we are planning and working hard to continue to grow our existing giving engines and to create more of them on our campus.

I am learning how crucial financial sustainability is to nonprofits. Nonprofits display the best of America and our local communities. People step out with a vision and a common purpose to impact lives. Nonprofits give birth to some of the greatest dreams and most noble causes. The National Council of Nonprofits states, "America's 1.3 million charitable nonprofits fund, heal, shelter, educate, inspire, enlighten, and nurture people of every age, gender, race, and socioeconomic status from coast to coast, border to border, and beyond."[x]

As great as their impact is, the greatest need for all of these nonprofits is sustainable funding. I have often heard the statistic that 80% of small businesses fail in the first five years. Most nonprofits suffer the same fate. They fail due to having insufficient funds or experiencing growth at an unsustainable pace. I have also read that "nearly 50% of nonprofits do not have cash reserves to cover next month's bills."[xi] This shows how crucial sustainable funding is for nonprofits.

Years ago, I listened to the late Billy Graham share about the Billy Graham Association. He asked the audience this question: "Do you know the most important thing I can do for the Association?"

As he paused, I thought about how I would respond to this question. I first thought that the greatest thing Billy Graham could do was preach the gospel. In his lifetime, it is estimated that he preached to 2.2 billion people, leading millions of them to Christ. My second thought was that he could write another book. He had already written thirty-three books. Or I thought that maybe the most important thing he could do would be to promote his radio program, "Hour of Decision" because it is carried on 700 stations worldwide.[xii] I also thought it would be important for him to train his staff and 10,000 volunteers.

But his answer caught my attention and helped me realize the incredible need nonprofits have. He said, "The most important thing I can do for the Billy Graham Association is to raise money because ministry needs funding." This doesn't sound real spiritual. But of all Billy Graham's amazing achievements, none of them could have been accomplished without raising money and without God's hand of provision.

Even though we all know this to be true, it helps me realize that as a leader, it is my responsibility to cast a vision so compelling that people want to be a part of it. When I was a young pastor, I had a good friend tell me, "Money follows vision! So, make your vision clear and cast it often."

God's Way of Answering Prayer

When it comes to praying for God to provide to meet our needs (whether for our personal lives or ministry operating costs), I would like to share how I've connected prayer and being part of the fundraising process. For years, I've taught on the topic of prayer. I often ask the class or small group, "How does God answer our prayers?"

Right away, I typically get three obvious answers:

1. God says, "Yes, right request and right time. I'll answer that!"

2. God says, "No, wrong request. You're asking with the wrong motives. There is just way too much of

you in this request." We see this explained in James 4:3: "When you ask, you do not receive, because you ask with wrong motives, that you may spend what you get on your pleasures."

3. God says, "Wait. It's the right request, but just not the right time."

   Then I ask the class, "Can you think of any other ways in which God might answer your prayers?"

   Usually, the group is silent and finally says, "Nope, I think that covers it."

4. I tell them that I used to think so too, and that for about twenty-five years, I taught these three answers. But in this last decade, I have realized that there are two more ways that God answers prayers. Here are my fourth and fifth additions.

5. God says, "Good request, but I'm not going to do that. I have a bigger, better idea." We see this in Isaiah 55:8–9: "'For my thoughts are not your thoughts, neither are your ways my ways,' declares the LORD. 'As the heavens are higher than the earth, so are my ways higher than your ways and my thoughts than your thoughts.'"

The last way God answers prayers is one we think He would not choose. God whispers His answer: "You do it! It's time for you to step out, step up, and do something with all the gifts, the talents, and the abilities I have given you. I put my Spirit in you, so you have my strength and power—it's all there for you."

Many years ago, I read a story that illustrates this point. A man had gone to the midweek prayer meeting at his church. When it was time to pray, he stood and prayed for his neighbor who had fallen on some hard times. This family needed food and other necessities. So he prayed the Lord would provide for them and meet their needs. Then he just stopped in the middle of his prayer and walked out of the service. Those who remained in the service continued to pray for quite a while. Once the meeting was over, most were standing around, talking, when the man walked back into the room. Someone who had noticed that he had abruptly left asked, "What happened? You were praying for your neighbor, and then you just stopped and walked out."

He said, "A strange thing happened. As I prayed for the Lord to meet my neighbor's needs, I heard the Lord tell me, 'You do it. You go get them some groceries.' So I did."

Did you know that praying can be a dangerous thing because God may say to you, "You do it"? God may say, "It's time. I have called you, equipped you, and provided for you. You go and be an answer to prayer."

One of our first outreach ministries to partner with us at the Hope Center was Light in Darkness, which was founded by Dr. Carolyn Knight. Carolyn told us about how the Lord led her to start this ministry. One day in 2005, she was driving by a billboard that advertised a strip club. It pictured a girl in fringed clothing with high stiletto boots in a provocative pose. The girl's eyes looked empty and sad.

On the spur of the moment, Carolyn prayed, "Oh, Lord, please send someone to help those young women."

To her surprise, the Lord spoke right back and said, "I found someone—it's you."

Carolyn said her stomach dropped because she didn't expect to hear that! But His voice was so clear, so she said yes and has never looked back. Today, she has thirty women's groups in six different states that go to strip clubs and other sex industry businesses to minister to the women working in them.[xiii]

Carolyn continues to lead her Light in Darkness ministry, but we are thrilled now to have Carolyn also as the Hope Center training manager and church liaison. She also helps recruit prayer warriors for our 24-hour prayer ministry. Today we have over 1,200 people committed to praying, with a goal of having 2,000 people praying every day for the healing of our residents and God's ongoing miracles and provisions.

Carolyn's story is just another example that when we pray, God may say to us, "You do it. It's your time to do something for me and my kingdom." This has spurred me to realize that when we were praying for God to provide for our financial needs at the Hope Center, He was telling us, "You can be involved in meeting this need too." That's when we started to pursue creating more giving engines to bring in income for the Hope Center ministry.

God's Economy

The question we need to ask and answer is *How do we practically carry out the concept of "You do it" and at the same time depend fully upon God to do it through us?* As we started the Hope Center, we had to roll up our sleeves and get to work. A lot of manual labor needed to be done—like painting our offices, cleaning carpets, and doing hundreds of other chores!

Earlier in this book, in chapter 5, I told the story of how a large pharmaceutical company offered Dave and me the opportunity to come to their building and pick out over thirty-five sets of solid-wood office furniture. Each office retailed at around $8,400. It seemed too good to be true! Then they ended up giving us twenty more sets of furniture plus a commercial kitchen set, which we gave away to an inner-city school that needed it. Altogether, their gift was worth around $500,000!

Let's consider this situation while asking the question, *How does God's economy work?* We did our part by getting the offices ready and by being willing to carry in nine semitrailers full of office furniture. And God did what He does best—He provided what we needed at the right time!

In Psalm 50:9–10 and 12, God says to the people of Israel, "I have no need of a bull from your stall or of goats from your pens, for every animal of the forest is mine, and the cattle on a thousand hills . . . If I were hungry, I would not tell you, for the world is mine, and all that is in it."

All the cattle on a thousand hills—it's God's. All the silver, all the gold, it's all God's. He's the Creator of all things, so all things are God's. I remember standing in our coffee shop at the Hope Center one day, and this lady introduced me to her friend. She said, "This is Pastor Hubert, and he owns the Hope Center."

I didn't want to embarrass her, but I said, "No, I'm just the person who helped start the Center. But Jesus owns the Hope Center. This is His ministry."

There needs to be a moment when we deed over our business or whatever we're holding to the Lord because He owns it anyway. For example, if we are church planters, then we acknowledge that the church plant is the Lord's, and it is up to God to make it grow. We must come to a point in our nonprofits, our personal lives, and whatever else we're leading, where it is not about us—it is all about Jesus. We must surrender all to the Lord and trust Him with it.

When it is about Him, and He is the owner of all of it, some amazing things begin to happen. We transfer that deed to him and place it in His care. Because He is the owner of everything, we can tap into His amazing resources.

Jesus didn't ever ask us to do everything in our own strength or by ourselves—not living the Christian life, not doing our everyday job, not parenting, not ministry. He always says, "I will be with you. I don't care where you are. To the ends of the earth, I'm going to be with you."

We're going to be co-laborers with God—did you hear that? You and I get to tag team with God so that God can use our lives to further the kingdom of God to rescue the perishing and make an eternal difference in people's lives. God never intended for us to do it alone. It's kind of like a three-legged race. If you've ever been in one, you know they tie your left leg to the right leg of the other runner. Then you try to run the race together. In Matthew 11:28–30, Jesus said it in this way: "Come to me, all you who are weary and burdened, and I will give you rest. Take my yoke upon you and learn from me, for I am gentle and humble in heart, and you will find rest for your souls. For my yoke is easy and my burden is light."

Jesus never tells you to do something and then just leaves you by yourself. He always wants to step into your business, nonprofit, and church. He wants to step into your life and your family. He wants to make sure that you understand something about Him. He is able to redeem, restore, renew, transform, and help all of us to see that He is the great provider.

I love seeing the miraculous provisions that only God could have brought about. I have a whole prayer journal of these incredible miracles of God that only can be explained by Him and what He has done.

But I also love when God says, "Hey, you do it. Just get in there, roll up your sleeves, and work hard for the kingdom of God. Go ahead, get out there and love the unlovable, the broken, and the hurting. And when you do that, you're loving like me. Just remember something, even though I say to you, 'You do it,' I will never leave you to do it by yourself."

Giving Engines at Hope Center Indy

Because the campus is so large, we were thinking, *What in the world have we gotten ourselves into? How will we build and sustain this ministry?* We felt a little overwhelmed, just like Moses when God asked him to lead his people out of Egypt to the promised land. In Exodus 4:1, Moses asked God some "what if" questions about things he thought might go wrong in Egypt. Moses asked, "*What if* they don't believe me? *What if* they don't listen to me? *What if* they say, 'The LORD did not appear to you'?"

I think we can all relate to Moses at times because we also want to ask God all the "what if" questions about everything that might go wrong. But notice what God says next to Moses.

In Exodus 4:2, the Lord asked Moses, "What is that in your hand?"

In Moses' hand was a shepherd's staff because he had been herding sheep. God took the shepherd's staff and turned it into the staff of God to perform the miracles Moses would need to set his people free.

When we are overwhelmed by the task God has given us, perhaps God asks us the same question: "What's in your hand?"

When I see that question, "What's in your hand?" it causes me to pause, remember that God has a plan, that He is way ahead of me, and to look at the people and resources that God has already placed in my life. Could it be that God has provided answers to all the "what if" questions before we realize it?

I have been reminded by my critics and my personal doubts on several occasions: I was in over my head with the Hope Center project. I had a friend share with me that a gentleman told him he believed Pastor Hubert had bit off more than he could chew with starting the Hope Center. My friend's response made me chuckle. He said, "I don't think Pastor Hubert gets to choose the size of his bite."

How true. God had chosen the project for us, and we to set out to accomplish it one bite at a time!

So with such a large undertaking, it caused us to look around at the assets on our campus, identify what we have, and brainstorm what we can do. When we did that, we realized we had this large entryway. As I shared in chapter 7, two volunteers turned our large entry into a beautiful boutique and coffee shop. They expanded the boutique business to include fundraisers like fashion shows and seasonal experiences people come to attend. As you know, they have now opened two more boutique locations. The boutique directors, Sarah and Rachel, along with their staff and volunteers, have used the gifts and abilities that God gave them—combined with a strong work ethic—to bring in significant income for the Hope Center each year.

There was another room in our lobby that Sarah and Rachel decided would be a great location for a beauty salon. They put together the business plan for the salon. It would have six booth spaces for hairstylists plus a side room for manicures and pedicures. Each of these spaces would be available for hairstylists to rent out. Churches and individuals gave money toward buying the equipment and sent volunteers to paint the space. Now the Hope Center receives the weekly rent income from the hairstylists, and our residents can get haircuts in this salon.

On our campus we also have a beautiful 5,000-square-foot brick barn that was built in 1892 and was used for woodworking before we took over the campus. In the early months after we moved onto the campus, I would take people on tours, and people would point to the barn and tell me, "This needs to be a wedding barn."

I agreed, "What a great idea!"

But I knew we would need a great team to run the event business for the barn. In 2017, the Wallace family stepped up to work together to clean out the barn, get the barn up to code as an event venue, and create the business plan for what we now call The Freedom Barn. To get this business off the ground, the Wallace family used the different gifts God gave them—administration, creative design, customer service, and even being a DJ—and combined them with the hard work of setup, teardown, and cleanup to make this giving engine successful for the Hope Center. The Freedom Barn held its first wedding in 2018, and now almost every week from April to October is booked with weddings and other events. Our HCI venue representatives are paid for working the weddings, and then the profit comes back to the Hope Center. Today The Freedom Barn is one of the Hope Center's profitable giving engines!

On our campus we also have a greenhouse. It's actually five greenhouses put together. When we first took over the campus, the roof had blown off, and it hadn't been used for about twenty years. Dave and I decided that we wanted to put the greenhouse back together. The owner of Heartland Nursery donated a new roof and had a crew put it on. Then a friend who has his degree in horticulture began to help us organize the greenhouse, so we could grow vegetables and flowers. Our greenhouse staff and volunteers use their "green thumbs" that God gave them to run our greenhouse business. Some of our residents have also enjoyed working in the greenhouse and seeing the beautiful flowers.

Another giving engine that I'm excited about is contract manufacturing that we are doing with 316 Product Development. 316 Product Development was one of our first partners at the Hope Center. The owner Jake Flagle and I have known each other since my days at Brookville Road Community Church. His heart to help extend God's kingdom fit with my heart to help women overcome life-threatening issues. Jake's business helps clients develop all sorts of products, including medical devices, electronics, consumer goods, automotive, and other products. Since Dave and I founded the Hope Center, Jake has come alongside our team to brainstorm about creating financial sustainability for the Hope Center.

One day in the fall of 2021, I was talking to Jake in the hallway by my office, and he shared his vision to open a new contract manufacturing business at the Hope Center as another giving engine. To do this, we would need to renovate a whole floor on one of our wings. We joked, "If we build it, they will come." It was all hands on deck to get the wing ready. We are proud to say 316 Product Manufacturing has now opened here at the Center. The Lord has faithfully provided our first group of customers, and new doors are opening almost weekly. The vision for 316 Product Manufacturing is fourfold: 1) To provide employment opportunities for our residents, 2) To help our residents discover their passion and use their God-given abilities, 3) To be a giving engine back to the Hope Center, 4) To provide world-class products to our customers. Our first resident to be hired full-time has been trained as an engineering technician. Her responsibilities have included soldering PCBs, making wiring harnesses, assembling electronics, leading assembly on a medical device build for clinical trials, setting up finished goods and distribution system, and managing a new state of the art high resolution biomedical 3D printer. Jake's heart for providing creative employment for the residents is starting to be fulfilled.

Now that we have our K9 Barn built on our campus, we are exploring options of creating another giving engine in the K9 Barn with providing related services, such as dog grooming and raising therapy dogs. We are looking into raising therapy dogs to sell to veterans and others who are looking to purchase a therapy dog to help support them through PTSD or various disabilities. Also, residents who like dogs will have the opportunity to be involved with the K9 program and take classes on caring for and training the dogs. This will be a "win-win," as working with the dogs will be comforting and fun for our residents. It will also give the residents and our team the purpose of being part of training therapy dogs that will serve people with PTSD and various disabilities.

Of course, being involved in the K9 program gives the residents and our team the purpose of helping with the dogs trained by Jordan Detection K9 to serve as electronic detection dogs who will assist law enforcement in child exploitation cases. My daughter Mary says that as she has talked to residents about the electronic detection dogs, she has heard them say that many of them still know others who are currently being trafficked, and they wish they could help them somehow, but they feel powerless to help. But working with the electronic detection dogs is one tangible way they get to fight trafficking and help other children get rescued from being exploited. This partnership with Jordan Detection K9 is an example of a partnership that only God could orchestrate!

Beating the Odds

All our giving engines not only help us with financial sustainability, but they also provide avenues for our residents to learn a variety of life skills on the job, because they have the opportunity to work in these businesses. While doing so, they develop skills in customer service, fashion design, being a barista, business administration, horticulture, event planning, dog training, and even entrepreneurship for those in some of our E.O.S. meetings. These on-campus businesses provide gainful employment for our residents while they are still on campus. The residents have managers who understand our program and are invested in making their job experience a growing experience—one they can add to their resumes. Our managers are happy to serve as professional references, as well.

When supporters of the Hope Center see how hard our team is working to not only do one-time fundraisers but to run businesses that serve as ongoing fundraisers, it seems they are more inclined to join us in our mission. They can see that our team is intentionally planning for long-term financial sustainability, and that causes them to believe that we can beat the odds of not making it as a nonprofit. Because they see us working hard, they are excited to support us financially and volunteer to help us do the work! Recently, as I was giving a tour, a lady said, "You guys don't just talk about doing something. You are actually getting things done!"

It is easy to talk about a vision and even write it down on paper. Too often when we write a vision with goals down, we think we have accomplished it. But to implement the vision and to see it happen takes another level of intentional focus. This is where so many fail: moving the vision from an idea to an accomplished dream.

To execute a vision, we must own the vision as a team, set short-term and long-term goals, and follow through on the action items on our team's weekly to-do list. We must be accountable to each other to do our part and see the vision through to completion. This hard work takes incredible spiritual energy and prayer to see the fruit of our labor.

Our Hope Center team is doing the work. We have never been accused of being slackers. I am so proud of our team and all who have come alongside us to help. On tours, I am often asked how long we have been running the Hope Center. I tell people, "Five years."

People often respond, "If you would have told me ten years or even longer, we would have believed you."

What has been done in the past five years is miraculous, and God's handprints are everywhere for all to see. As a team, we have felt so blessed to have been on this journey together and to see God's wonderful provisions. There is so much more to be done, and we will keep our eyes on greater things so we can have an impact well into the future.

I don't know the vision God has put in your heart, or if He has said, "I have gifted you, empowered you, so you do it." But whatever it is, remember He will help you accomplish it. It is our prayer that you can say if God can do it for the Hope Center, He can do it for me! Yes, He can, so you do it!

Promises to Read:

Psalm 50:9–10, 12: "I have no need of a bull from your stall or of goats from your pens, for every animal of the forest is mine and the cattle on a thousand hills. If I were hungry, I would not tell you, for the world is mine, and all that is in it."

Matthew 28:20: "And surely I am with you always, to the very end of the age."

Ephesians 3:20-21: "Now to Him who is able to do immeasurably more than all we ask or imagine, according to His power that is at work within us, to Him be glory in the church and in Christ Jesus throughout all generations, for ever and ever! Amen."

Prayer to Pray:

Jesus, I want to do something to help in your kingdom. Would You share an idea, a purpose, Your leading to help me discern your direction? Take my gifts and use them for Your ministry to help others. In Jesus' name, Amen.

Redefined Hope Boutique at the Morristown location

Commercial Sign on the road to invite people to shop at our giving engines

Greenhouse

Freedom Barn wedding venue

14

Running with Hope

In my office, I have a plaque picturing an older runner. (He looks like he might be going on 67 years old, just like me!) Under the runner are the words from Philippians 3:13-14: "Forgetting what is behind and straining toward what is ahead, I press on toward the goal to win the prize for which God has called me heavenward in Christ Jesus." Like that runner persevering in a race, I want to run my race well and finish strong right up to the day I go to heaven.

In 2011, Tonia and I ran a marathon together. As we were 54 and 56 at the time, we do use the word *run* loosely. We trained six days a week for about four months, walking and jogging several miles together on the country roads by our house. On the day of the marathon, we set out to run the 26.2 miles. The marathon directors had a "wimpy bus" (as people would call it) to drive along the route to pick up any of the runners who were sick, injured, or felt they couldn't finish. Tonia pulled a muscle in her leg on mile 21 and was in a great deal of pain, but she refused to stop until we reached the finish line. There was no ride back on the wimpy bus for us. We finished, not strong--but rejoicing. Our time of six hours and 24 minutes broke no record for our age group, but we joke that it did break us.

Yet kidding aside, I want to keep running the race of life and finish well. I will be turning 67 soon. I need to keep believing God's promises. To do that, I must let hope fill my heart and have eyes of faith to keep running and not stop.

Maybe you have heard it said, "The speed of the leader becomes the speed of the organization." If, as leaders, we stop running and sit down, everyone we are leading tends to sit down too. Through every challenge we have experienced in the past several years, I have been determined to keep standing on God's promises instead of sitting down in discouragement. I want my family and the people looking to me for leadership in our organization to know that there's no recliner in my immediate future (except for my Sunday afternoon naps!).

Setting Goals

This is why we need to dream dreams and set goals to help us run at a good pace. Years ago, I read the adage, "We never plan to fail; we just fail to plan." This helped shape my God-given direction. It helped me to understand that planning was a major part of accomplishing God's purpose for my life. Over 25 years ago, I tried to write out 100 goals for my life. I got this idea from an article about the Hall of Fame college football coach Lou Holtz. In 1966 Holtz had just lost his assistant coaching job at the University of South Carolina. Instead of feeling distraught about losing that job, he wrote out 107 goals for his life. (When he shared them with his wife, she told him to add one more goal--get a new job!) One of his audacious goals was to win a national championship, which he did at Notre Dame in 1988. Some of his other goals were to meet the U.S. president, meet the Pope, and be on *The Tonight Show*. He accomplished all of these. From the last update I read, Holtz had achieved 103 of the 107 goals he had set.[xiv]

Holtz's vision and desire to achieve inspired me to write out 100 goals for my life. My first goal was to write out 100 goals, which I found to be a difficult task. After a month of praying, thinking through dreams, and discussing them with my wife, I completed my list. Some goals were spiritual, financial, family-oriented, career-oriented, etc. Over the years I have fine-tuned them. Even though at times, I have

263

set some aside, I have always kept my eyes on these goals. One of my goals was to write a book--which I am accomplishing with this book!

I remember as a young pastor that one of my financial goals was to give a million dollars to missions. One Sunday morning during my message, I confessed my goal to the church. To tell others makes us accountable and keeps it at the top of our prayer list. As crazy as it sounded and unsure how this could happen, I still proclaimed my desire for this goal. On the way home from church that day, my daughter Sara said, "Dad, I believe you are going to accomplish this goal of giving away a million dollars to missions." I loved her faith in me as a leader, but even more how she believed God would bring it to pass. Today I'm well on my way to accomplishing this goal, and the finish line is in sight. Now I need a larger goal for giving and to keep running with greater faith.

Because of our church's ministry partnership with Pastor Tele Moraes in Brazil, another one of my goals was to help plant 100 churches in Northeast Brazil. Today 37 churches have been planted or are in the early stages of being planted. One of our family goals was for me to take all of our children on a short-term mission trip, and I was able to do that multiple times. So a new goal for us is for my wife and I to get all our grandchildren on the mission field. Next summer we hope to take some of our older granddaughters to Brazil to participate in a 30-year celebration of the ministry we have been part of since my early days of pastoring Brookville Road Community Church.

Another goal was to do ministry with my wife. During all the mission trips I had with our children, Tonia wanted to stay home to take care of the other children. Now that our children are grown, we're excited to travel together to do ministry abroad. We were able to go to Israel a couple years ago. The year after David's passing, we were able to do ministry with David's wife, Stephanie, in India. In just over a month, we are on our way to Africa to encourage believers and church leaders. We hope to go on a safari and see some other wonderful sights. If you would have told me in my early years of ministry that I would go on 30-40 mission trips around the world, I would have said, "That is crazy thinking." But life and ministry are an adventure with God so let's keep running and see where He leads us. Tonia and I really enjoy traveling together and serving together at the Hope Center, where she leads prayer groups, mentors women, helps with special events, and serves in many other ways as needs arise.

Lou Holtz's percentage of accomplishments from his list of goals is very impressive. We may not have that same percentage. Some goals that you and I set are so big that they may never be reached in our lifetime, but they still help present a big target for us to aim at. Goals give long-term vision and short-term energy to help us make decisions that lead us toward our desired future. If you want to take the challenge to write out 100 goals for your life, let me encourage you to go for it! Maybe your first goal is to write 100 goals (or maybe just start with ten!).

Goals for Hope Center's Future

Our Hope Center team also sees the importance of setting goals. Following the E.O.S. process (which I referred to in chapter 11), our Hope Center executive team and department teams set new 90-day "rocks" every quarter. These "rocks" are specific goals we are prioritizing to complete in that quarter. Every week our team members are accountable for sharing whether they are on track or off track with their goals. The E.O.S. standard is for teams to accomplish 80% of their quarterly goals. Last quarter our executive team accomplished 91% of their goals. It amazes me how much we can get done when we intentionally discuss which goals to set as a team and then hold each other accountable to work on our goals to complete them by the deadline. Then we do it all over again at the start of every quarter. I am so proud of all the department teams at the Hope Center because they are focused on doing quality work, growing the ministry, and accomplishing our mission of imparting hope and healing to our residents, other staff, volunteers, and all who journey onto the Hope Center campus. There is so much more we can and want to accomplish for our Lord. The Hope Center is so young, just over five years old, and her future is bright. Her greatest days are ahead of her as we keep running the race.

One of the goals that I'm excited about for the Hope Center is to grow our various compassion ministries to impact our community. One of these compassion ministries is the David Nolen Pantry of Hope. After David's homegoing in 2019, we were approached by the grocery chain Kroger to create a food pantry in David's memory. We were told that 20% of families in our county struggle with food scarcity. As a family, we felt this was so honoring to David's memory and wanted to be a blessing for those in our community who need food. Kroger donated $15,000 and committed to giving quarterly to keep the shelves stocked. On October 16, 2019, we cut the ribbon on the David Nolen Pantry of Hope. We are so grateful for the several community partners who have teamed up with us to provide needed resources to help us meet the growing demand for food in our community. I can't thank our food pantry director Michelle Gambrel and her husband, Greg, enough for all their hard work and tireless commitment to oversee the 70 volunteers who serve weekly to bring food in, sort it, and carry it out each Thursday evening to the families who come for food. Since our opening with all our partners and volunteers, we have given away 1.75 million pounds of food. Right now we're setting a goal to have a greater impact on our community by building a separate building to expand the food pantry and create a farmer's market to produce fresh vegetables. This is certainly in the dream stage right now, but we have written down the proposal and are waiting to see what God will do.

As I write this chapter, I'm looking out the window and seeing the electronic detection dogs being trained on our campus and getting ready for their graduation tomorrow morning. These seven dogs graduating tomorrow are joining the list of the other 83 dogs trained by Jordan Detection K9 and deployed all over the U.S. to assist law enforcement. I paused to think about what these dogs will accomplish in the fight against child exploitation. The latest statistic from Operation Underground Railroad is that the 41 dogs that O.U.R. sponsored with Jordan Detection K9 for the time period of January 1, 2022, through August 1, 2022, is the 41 dogs made 226 arrests and rescued 51 children. Incredible! These are just half of the dogs that have been trained by Jordan Detection K9, so those numbers could very well be doubled if all the dogs' arrests and rescues were included in the data. Just thinking about these dogs and their amazing handlers caused me to tear up and be so thankful we are in this fight together against human trafficking. Todd Jordan's goal is to have one of these dogs in every state. Today we have dogs in 32 states, so we have 18 to go!

Our co-founder David said, "Let's pray and ask God to create a Hope Center in all 50 states." If our Lord tarries, I may not live to see these centers, but others will. God will call amazing people who I don't even know to create other Hope Centers in other states. He will call these Christ-followers to carry the baton of hope and hand it to another generation. Maybe that's you! You will set the pace for a new generation of hope runners. Let us refuse to get on the wimpy bus and run in such a way to win the prize for which God has called us heavenward in Christ Jesus. Those greater days I speak of for the Hope Center will only happen if you join us in this race, in this fight, on this day in which we have been called to stand up and be counted.

Running as a Hope Dealer

Several years ago, I pulled into a parking lot of a large box store. When I parked, I saw a truck with an eye-catching paint job with these words painted on the front doors of both the driver and the passenger sides: "Hope Dealers." The truck belonged to a recovery ministry for those struggling with addictions. I thought, *How appropriate! It wasn't Dope Dealers; it was Hope Dealers.*

As I admired the slogan, I thought, *I wish I had thought of that.* It's so clever and so true. We are all dealers in one way or another. We either deal out hopelessness, or we give our lives to be Hope Dealers.

After I gave my life to Christ and was filled with His blessed hope of eternal life, I wanted to share this good news with everyone I could. I pray over these last forty-six years I have been a relentless hope dealer. My life has been a marathon of hope, where I have been given the divine privilege to pass on hope to everyone I have met on my life run.

Our life of hope is a book with many chapters. Some of those chapters are written with great joy, while others are written with tears. How we find our way in the darkest night or when the sun is shining is our story. Every moment along the way shaped our lives and revealed to us the hope that was readily available and desperately needed. It is your story, whether you have embraced the hope Christ freely offered or whether you have refused it. If you still have doubts, why don't you just give hope a try? By this time in your life, maybe you have tried everything else, and it has only left you feeling empty. The hope of Christ is the greatest gift you can ever receive. His hope is the power needed to get back up again when life has knocked you down and to keep running a life with hope.

After reading this book, I hope you say to yourself, *If God can use a pig farmer, He can surely use me.* Let me say to you, "Go for it! Allow God to use your one and only life for Him. Go on. Go on. Believe God's promises and become for Him a Hope Dealer!"

Promises to Read

Romans 15:13: "May the God of hope fill you with all joy and peace as you trust in him, so that you may overflow with hope by the power of the Holy Spirit."

Philippians 3:13-14: "Brothers and sisters, I do not consider myself yet to have taken hold of it. But one thing I do: Forgetting what is behind and straining toward what is ahead, I press on toward the goal to win the prize for which God has called me heavenward in Christ Jesus."

Hebrews 12:1-2: "Therefore, since we are surrounded by such a great cloud of witnesses, let us throw off everything that hinders and the sin that so easily entangles. And let us run with perseverance the race marked out for us, fixing our eyes on Jesus, the pioneer and perfector of faith."

Prayers to Pray

Heavenly Father, thank You for everyone who has read Hope for a Lifetime! I ask for all of them You will give them the same hope You have given me and the Nolen family! Please plant in their hearts a faith to run the race and finish well. Take them on an adventure of a lifetime. In Jesus' name, Amen.

Connecting to Hope Center Indy

If this book has impacted your life, we'd love to hear from you! You can contact us directly at hope@hopecenterindy.org or 317-752-1500. To connect to Hope Center Indy, go to hopecenterindy.org. There you can also subscribe to our monthly newsletter, sign up for a campus tour, request a speaker for an event, listen to our podcast, consider ways to volunteer, donate online, shop at our businesses, and more. If you are on social media, I encourage you to follow the Hope Center Indy Facebook page, Instagram page, YouTube channel, and/or LinkedIn profile. Thank you for your support!

Ethical Storytelling Guidelines

Our Hope Center Indy executive team has worked hard over the past year to develop Ethical Storytelling Guidelines when it comes to stewarding the stories of current and former residents. These are some of the careful considerations we took in the collection and sharing of the survivor stories contained in this book:

- All stories are shared with explicit and informed consent from the owners of those stories,
- The graduates wrote their own stories and were engaged throughout the book's editing process,
- The graduates are fully aware of our wide intended audiences and agree in sharing their stories as a way

to freely express how God has changed their lives through a personal relationship with Him, to raise awareness and education, and to inspire other survivors that healing is possible,

- The graduates agree and support that the proceeds from the sale of this book help raise funds to support the healing journey of other women enrolled in our programs,
- The graduates were in complete control of their narratives and shared only aspects of their stories that they were comfortable with,
- The graduates were encouraged to use discretion to protect themselves, their loved ones, and their personal information,
- The graduates chose how they wished to be recognized and identified in their stories.

The women who shared their stories in this book have inspired many of our staff and volunteers. We know that they will inspire countless more.

Acknowledgments

No book is written or lived alone. I want to thank my beautiful wife, Tonia, and our wonderful children, Sara, Rachel, Shari, Mary, and David who brought joy and laughter into all our lives.

I want to especially thank our youngest daughter, Mary, who with long-suffering worked on this book with me to correct my literary weaknesses. For all your time and hard work, I am so grateful. You are a blessing to me and to so many others.

I also want to thank Andy Flink for his willingness to read the first rough copies of the chapters with Mary and me and give his feedback. Thank you to our editor Christina Pfister for the insights she gave during the developmental edit and the copy edit. I would like to thank Sara Feasel, who gave input at all stages of writing the book and used her creative design for the book cover, the timeline, and the photos included in the book. Thank you to Sandra Cabrera for her willingness to read and review several chapters as we were trying to finalize the manuscript. Thank you to Josh Bach for setting up the studio for me to record the audiobook, listening to me read the book aloud, and editing the files for the audiobook. And thank you to the Hope

Center graduates who bravely shared their stories! You all helped bring this book to life!

To all our family, friends, and brothers and sisters in Christ who have been part of our hope journey, we have been so blessed to have walked with you. Thank you for your investment in this hog farmer turned Christ follower. For all of you, I am forever indebted and eternally blessed. You are loved.

About the Author

Pastor Hubert Nolen is the co-founding executive director of Hope Center Indy. He is the former senior pastor of Brookville Road Community Church in New Palestine, IN, a church he led for 33 years. Under Pastor Hubert's leadership, the church provided millions to world missions and church planting. He was instrumental in establishing more than 70 churches globally, including in India and Brazil. He earned his bachelor's degree in Bible and Pastoral Ministry from Barclay College and completed graduate studies at Asbury Seminary and Trinity Evangelical

Seminary. After becoming aware of the need in 2015, Pastor Nolen was compelled to launch a center where victims of human trafficking from coast to coast and from all walks of life could find a place to heal and recover from the effects of human trafficking. He and his wife, Tonia, have been married 40+ years. They have five children, thirteen grandchildren, two great-grandchildren, and live on their family farm in Indiana.

Notes

Chapter:3

[i] Coxe Bailey, Faith. (1958). *George Mueller: He Dared to Trust God for the Needs of Countless Orphans*. The Moody Bible Institute: Chicago.

Chapter:5

[ii] "Dream Center." Accessed on July 27, 2022. https://www.dreamcenter.org.

[iii] "Sex Trafficking." Polaris. Accessed on July 29, 2022. https://humantraffickinghotline.org/type-trafficking/sex-trafficking.

[iv] "2019 Data Report: The U.S. National Human Trafficking Hotline." Polaris. Accessed on July 29, 2022. https://polarisproject.org/wp-content/uploads/2019/09/Polaris-2019-US-National-Human-Trafficking-Hotline-Data-Report.pdf

[v] "2019 Data Report: The U.S. National Human Trafficking Hotline." Polaris. Accessed on July 29, 2022. https://polarisproject.org/wp-content/uploads/2019/09/Polaris-2019-US-National-Human-Trafficking-Hotline-Data-Report.pdf.

[vi] (2022). "Vulnerabilities & Recruitment." Polaris. Accessed on July 29, 2022. https://polarisproject.org/recognizing-human-trafficking-vulnerabilities-recruitment.

[vii] (2022). The Samaritan Women Institute for Shelter Care. Accessed on July 29, 2022. https://thesamaritanwomen.org/video-2020.

Chapter:8

[viii] (2014). "Song Story: '10,000 Reasons' By Matt Redman." *Worship Leader*. Accessed on August 5, 2022. https://worshipleader.com/culture/10000-reasons-by-matt-redman/.

Chapter:12

[ix] Operation Underground Railroad. "What We Do." Accessed on August 9, 2022. https://www.ourrescue.org.

Chapter:13

[x] (2022). National Council of Nonprofits. "Nonprofit Impact in Communities." Accessed on August 12, 2022. https://www.councilofnonprofits.org/nonprofit-impact-communities.

[xi] (2022.) The Hope Center. "Challenges That Nonprofits Face." Accessed on August 9, 2022.

https://www.thehopecenter.org/?fbclid=IwAR0oN0gGbEpHHy3qSsINl
QbV2Hm-GooiAHKTTVysdubujMMpLKdY1dz0chk.

[xii] (2018). "Billy Graham's Life & Ministry By the Numbers." *Lifeway Research*. Accessed on August 12, 2022.
https://research.lifeway.com/2018/02/21/billy-grahams-life-ministry-by-the-numbers/.

[xiii] Light in Darkness. "About." Retrieved on August 22, 2022.
https://lightindarknessministry.com/how-the-ministry-began/.

Chapter:14

[xiv] White, Paul. (1997). "Holtz's Message: Set Your Goals and Never Give Up Hope." *The Virginian Pilot*. Accessed on September 8, 2022.
https://scholar.lib.vt.edu/VA-news/VA-Pilot/issues/1997/vp970109/01090524.htm.